Irwin Edman

AS a freshman in high school, Irwin Edman, already dubbed "Professor" by his contemporaries, first gained local fame by reciting "The Ancient Mariner" complete after reading it but once. Today hundreds of Columbia alumni can tell corroborating tales of Dr. Edman's fabulous memory—tales which, strangely enough, are mixed with others designed to paint him as the prototype of the absent-minded professor. But these feats of memory and prodigies of forgetfulness, astounding or amusing as they may be, are less important than the fact that Irwin Edman has made of philosophy one of the most popular and rewarding subjects in the university. He has a faculty for taking the ideas out of the books he knows so well and making them live forever in the minds of his students. In 1938, at the age of 42 one of the youngest of full professors, he wields an intellectual influence not accounted for by his years.

A number of books related to philosophy have come from Dr. Edman's pen, but he is by no means limited to this field. He has contributed frequent articles to the *New York Herald Tribune, The New Republic, The Nation, Saturday Review of Literature,* and other newspapers and magazines. He is one of the most faithful supporters of F.P.A.'s *Conning Tower,* producing for that famous column a quantity of excellent topical verse.

Dr. Edman lives on Morningside Heights, and he may be seen almost any fine day striding up Riverside Drive or drinking coffee in some shop on upper Broadway. But he may be found as well at Carnegie Hall or in the Museum of Modern Art, and there are few places in America or Europe where his figure has not been a familiar sight. Dr. Edman, indeed, is at home in the world, and it is for that reason that he writes with such charm, such humor, and such lasting good sense about the people who inhabit it.

Philosopher's Holiday

IRWIN EDMAN

NEW YORK

The Viking Press

MCMXXXVIII

First published in November 1938

TO

META *and* LESTER

And therefore the mind of the philosopher alone has wings; and this is just, for he is always, according to the measure of his abilities, clinging in recollection to those things in which God abides, and in beholding which he is what he is.

—PLATO, *Phædrus*

Contents

x Contents

Philosopher's Holiday

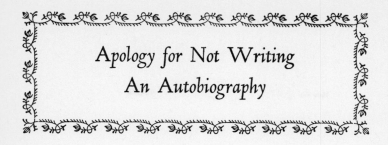

Apology for Not Writing
An Autobiography

THERE are many good reasons for writing autobiography these days, or there are many good reasons alleged. Everybody has been something: an infantry officer, a foxhunting man, a prisoner, a prison-warden, an author, a publisher, a President, a President's wife, a foreign correspondent, a prep school boy, a baby. One enterprising baby of my acquaintance has already arranged to publish his memoirs in co-operation with a famous psycho-analyst as soon as each of them has learned to write intelligible English. Perhaps the most important autobiography of our era would be the Personal History of a Nobody-at-all. For have we not been repeatedly informed by competent social critics that our age is one of impotent nobodies hurtling toward nothingness? Would not the Personal History of a Nobody-at-all be accurately hailed by discerning critics as the most characteristic summary of our epoch? I had thought of writing such a book. But, in the first place, I have been assured that there are already dozens of volumes, published under titles less candid, which exactly fill that niche. And, after all, I am somebody: radio surveys call me up and ask me what programme I have been listening to.

It is, therefore, a great temptation to put down in searing and dramatic accents the story of my spiritual unfolding. It could neatly be classified as an American Testament, an American Idyll, an American Education, or, given the current psychiatric fashions, an American Neurosis. But I refrain. Not, I confess, with ease. For I, too, have had a childhood, morbidly happy on the surface but full of horror and perversion underneath, unknown to my family or to myself. But it appears now that Freud knew about it all along. I grew up in the years from 1900 to 1910 in simple, *gemütlich* Manhattan, through which one could cheerfully ride a bicycle from the farms in outlying Harlem to Forty-Second Street and Fifth Avenue. I knew that friendly, simple town (as it now seems) full of brownstone houses (which I did not know were the ugly exteriors of cramped bourgeois lives) and German beer gardens, penny arcades, and nickelodeons, and I saw it metamorphosed into megalopolitan New York. There could really be some charming sketches of the open-air trolleys that took one on exciting adventures to Fort George or Coney Island, of the neighbours whom one actually *knew*, of shouting "Get a horse" to goggled automobilists in rare and precarious automobiles, of games of "cops and robbers," of nice boys in starched collars and toughs with no collars at all whom we nice boys feared and admired. Something of all that may, despite myself, creep into these pages—autobiography or no.

Then there were the war years which, by a chronological accident, I spent at college. Those were the hopeful early days of pacifico-liberalism when H. G. Wells was our major prophet, Galsworthy and Bennett our major novelists, and Walter Lippmann's *Preface to Politics* the promising manifesto of the bright young men. We quoted Rupert Brooke's "If I should die, think only this of me," and "These hearts were woven of human joys and cares, Washed marvellously with sorrow, swift to mirth"; we read and wept over Cornelia Stratton Parker's *American Idyll;* we thought that *The Research Magnificent* (the title of one of Wells's novels) was to give us that brave new world which we did not know was going to be the satirical title of another novel, by Aldous Huxley, unknown to us, one of our contemporaries. The *New Republic* had begun to make pronouncements, majestic and lucid, many of them by Walter Lippmann; a renascence in American poetry was announced and supposedly illustrated by Louis Untermeyer; the war came as a pleasantly distant excitement in a Europe that seemed psychically much more than three thousand miles away.

Then, too, I have been for some twenty years now a teacher of philosophy and have seen a whole parade and cycle of types and varieties of youth. I told all about that once in a relatively learned article in the Sunday *Times.* Put in a pronoun here and there, make it a little more personal and a little less pontifical, and it would make a creditable section of the Testament of a Teacher. I can hardly refrain from writing that chapter, for it seems to me nobody has quite succeeded in putting into print the bitter-sweet pleasures of teaching, the joys of making things clear and making them vivid, or appearing to do so, to the receptive, or to the apparently receptive, young. No one has yet translated into words the curious emotion that comes from seeing what happens afterwards in the way of hard-boiled success-hunting or success-having to the finer-tempered among the youths one has taught. There would be a wry section on Former Students, and the wriest part of it would probably be about the successes.

There would be a passage, too, on the mavericks among students, the shining or eccentric solitaries and exceptions. There would be the boy who performed the Black Mass and got married at seventeen; the æsthete who fled to the highlands of Jamaica and when last heard from was still there. There would be the story of the young man who came out of Alabama with the drawl of the deep South in his voice and, before he got his degree, the dedication of the deep revolutionary in his heart and the star in his destiny of becoming the secretary of the Communist Party in a large conservative Southern city. There would be something about the jester who became a Jesuit, and the gentle freshman who became a well-known legal Nemesis of gangsters, and the very correct young man who became a kind of gangster himself.

Then there would be a good deal about the run-of-the-mill student, and something about the failure of all education and of the failure of all else if education is a failure.

And then—I had almost forgotten—there would be the Memoirs of a Music-Lover. I have spent a long life, if it were all put together, in Carnegie Hall, and many years, were the hours placed end to end, listening to the radio or to records and to amateur musicians. Hardly a man is now alive —but I am he—who remembers the Sunday evening in Carnegie Hall when George Antheil's *Ballet Mécanique* was produced, all the world and his wife, including many who had never been to a concert before, being gathered to hear the

New Note in music. The New Note seemed to be chiefly the shaking of a sheet of tin, as part of the orchestration, the sheet of tin being shaken by a former student of mine. All industrial civilization was said to be epitomized in the work, and much of its noise was.

I have lived to see Sibelius pass, in the opinion of the public and of myself, from something strange and difficult, an assault on musical comfort, to something as familiar and sometimes as banal as Tchaikovsky. I have heard the Philharmonic conducted by metronomes under contract and by Toscanini, and have lived to see the phonograph pass from a contraption wheezy and blaring—for which every music-lover had contempt—to the pride of connoisseurs with collectors' items in the way of records of sixteenth-century music; and the same snobbishness developed about the collection of records that used to go to ignoring them. Along with others I scorned the radio and find it difficult now to resist its constant musical temptations; and have lived from the days when you were lucky to hear Beethoven played four hands on the piano, to the epoch when you can hear it day and night over some radio station or other. And in such a memoir there would be the opportunity and the temptation to reflect on the strange hold music has on the intellectual class, who find in it something they cannot find in the brittle hardness of words and a peace they cannot find in the distracting discords, literal and spiritual, of the post-war world.

There are other possible chapters, too, for a not impossible autobiography: the post-war young American in Europe finding in ancient monuments the opening of his imaginative eyes, and in ancient cities the liberation of his spirit, or perhaps only the excitement of his senses. I don't think that chapter would need to be written. It could be pasted together from a dozen other autobiographies, many of whose authors are now settled on farms in Connecticut and Vermont.

Or I could call the book *A Traveller's Tale*. Leaving out the long periods when I have been at home and at my job, it would not be hard to make it an account of a life that seemed to consist entirely of being on transatlantic steamers, on trains in the West, in pensions and hotels on the Continent, in lodgings at Oxford, visiting friends in the quiet English countryside or in a village amid the tranquil cows and grass of the Dutch fields that (such is the power of art) all looked like Ruysdaels to me. That section would be filled with such glimpses as are opened to the traveller's or the visitor's eye. There would be no startling adventures, for I have had none, save with a confidence man in France who swindled me by a pathetic and convincing plea for fifty dollars. There would be no battlefronts, no or few encounters with the great, though I should not be able to resist a vignette of Havelock Ellis in a wilderness of papers in his London flat, or of Bergson speaking in immaculate English in his quiet apartment in Paris. There would be no revelations of the inside of Europe, no scarlet excitements about transgressions, no speaking plainly and as I pleased about the private side of public regimes. There would be glimpses here and there of a poet encountered in the form of the owner of a pewter shop in Belgium; pleasant little encounters with simple families in the Schwarzwald or in Devon; the French merchant met in an Arab restaurant near Beirut who had retired from business to make a grand tour and recite Renan's "Prayer on the Acropolis" on the spot. There would be the exciting beauty of pictures and churches when first I saw them in Europe, and the uneasiness at seeing the quiet which one had found in Europe come to seem (as one came to know Europe better) but the illusion of the eye of the traveller with no responsibilities but that of enjoyment and the thoughts of a wanderer whose head was full of the past rather than of the present. Were I to write that chapter *in extenso,* I should have some moralizings on the eye of the traveller as the ideal instrument of detached observation, and something about the traveller's way being the way to go through life. Save that in life one is not detached and the traveller's eye as often gives him images rather than insights, unless he learns in time to be more than a traveller.

There could be a chapter, too, on post-war literary society, the cocktail parties at which, being prevented by a bad digestion from partaking of many cocktails, I was enabled, perhaps with more detachment, to observe the temper and thoughts of those who did. There would be memories of the great; one can hardly live in New York in academic and literary circles without meeting a few of them, and acquiring incidentally a rough-and-ready measure of distinguishing the real thing from the counterfeit.

And, finally, there would be a chapter on the history of my ideas, or the ideas I picked up as I lived along with articulate friends and the liberal weeklies. There would be reflections on the post-war liberal and the post-war revolutionary, and considerations on the difference between revolution in word and in fact, and the way in which words themselves, where conversation is rampant, become, as they did in sophisticated circles in ancient Athens, the substitute for ideas, aphrodisiacs of the spirit.

I do not guarantee that none of these things will creep into these pages; and reminiscent reflection is bound to be, however indirectly, autobiography. But this book is not a Testament, nor an Education, nor a Personal History, great as is the temptation, now that I have begun to think about it, to produce some such work. I propose, however, simply to set down, more or less in the order in which they occur to me, impressions of persons and places, many of them obscure, about which I have occasionally told my friends over a glass of sherry, sometimes to their amusement—and when the sherry was good, to their edification—or at least I so imagined. A professional training as a philosopher leads one to interlard stories with principles and to make stories sometimes carry morals. But enough of preface. If the reader will find himself a glass of sherry, I should like to begin by telling him about M. Platon.

ONE

M. Platon

"You had better come with us to Italy," said my friends as I left them at Vézelay, where the grandiose Abbaye and its superb spaces and capitals and the June weather and the pleasures of reunion (I had been away a year) had given us a very good time together.

"No, I have made up my mind to see Autun," I insisted. "There's a fine Romanesque cathedral there." And I began to recite its simple unadorned charm, its historical importance, the beauty of the surrounding country, the Roman theatre where the Comédie Française came to play in the summer. I had been reading the *Guide Bleu* with care.

I knew I had made no mistake even before seeing the cathedral, for the Hôtel St.-Louis was one of those inns on the Continent which make one find a reason for staying in a town longer than one had intended. It was then well over a hundred years old; they show you the room where Napoleon slept. It has an inner courtyard where the stage-coaches and carriages used to draw up. My room under the eaves seemed singularly homelike and comfortable and had a bath, which

Napoleon's room did not. I arrived late in the afternoon and had a glimpse of the cathedral before dark. The *Guide Bleu* had not exaggerated. I took a walk out of town through rolling green country that reminded me at once of the Cotswolds and of Vermont. "This," I said to myself, "is just the place to stay for a couple of weeks of reading and writing."

I was sure of it that night at dinner. Apparently Autun was now on one of the main motor roads to the South, and for all its sleepy, comforting isolation had a good deal of passing tourist traffic. The *cuisine* was *renommée*. So was the wine. I was lonely without my friends and drank considerable of it. I felt wonderful. "Why did nobody tell me of Autun before?" I thought as I was falling asleep.

Next morning I wished I had never heard of it. The *cuisine renommée*, the *vin superbe*, had done for me. I was sure I had ptomaine poisoning. I asked the *valet de chambre* to send the friendly manager, whom the evening before I had complimented on his food, his wine, his country, and the room that Napoleon had slept in.

"Is it," I said wanly when he appeared, "that there is a doctor in Autun?"

"But yes, monsieur," he said briskly. "M. Platon."

"But you are joking, monsieur, *c'est de la blague,* not really M. Platon." Even though I had ptomaine poisoning, I wouldn't believe there was anybody named Plato in a French provincial town.

"Yes, M. Platon," the innkeeper said simply, "an excellent family physician; he has attended my own family for twenty years now; a physician of the first order."

"Send M. Platon," I said weakly, wondering whether ptomaine poisoning was fatal. I remembered that Aristotle, anyway, was a physician and that there was a good deal about the humours of the body in Plato; and a physician, Erixymachus, appears in one of the dialogues. Maybe this Platon chap was all right after all.

Twenty minutes later—I was growing more and more sure it was ptomaine poisoning—I heard a hearty voice down the corridor. "*Alors,* where is the American?" The voice sounded almost threatening. Perhaps these provincial doctors still believed in blood-letting.

There entered my room not the diminutive Frenchman I had somehow expected but a tall, heavy man with bushy hair and eyebrows (he turned out to have originated in the Basque country); very brisk and energetic in his movements and an impatient firmness in his eye. He looked not at all like the busts of Plato, though he did have a broad brow.

"If you will permit me, sir," he said, and, much to my surprise, took from my table some galley-proofs of the *Journal of Philosophy* that I had hoped to read in the course of the morning. *Journal of Philosophy* was printed at the top of each galley.

"English," he said, pointing accusingly to the innocent words, "is simply French badly spelt. I do not, monsieur, speak English, or, as I could easily demonstrate, not very well. I do not read it very well either. But I read it well enough to see that English is simply French badly spelt and badly pronounced, and badly constructed. *Journal de la Philosophie, n'est-ce pas?* Monsieur, I am a philosopher not only in name but in nature. You must translate that article for me. It seems to be something that concerns the æsthetic. Is it, perhaps, your own?"

"Yes, monsieur."

"Then all the more reason: translate it for me at once."

"But, doctor, I am not feeling very well," I protested. Sight translation, or second sight translation, of even one's own prose in the midst of an attack of ptomaine poisoning was not a project that captured my imagination for the moment. Yet M. Platon looked menacing, and, after all, the request was an unexpected compliment from an unexpected source.

The doctor sat down by my bedside and I proceeded in a feeble voice—and, I fear, rather feeble French—to translate my ideas, which had, as I remember it, something to do with the relations of poetry and philosophy. M. Platon listened attentively. At the end of the third galley, I looked up, hoping for a respite.

"Continue, monsieur, there are points on which I do not agree, but it is well written." (I was vaguely reminded of meetings of the Philosophy Club to which I belong and where I had heard that sort of thing from polite fellow-members.)

There were five galleys and I was not allowed to stop until I had translated them all.

"You have certain nuances of construction that are not exactly French," he said, "but on the whole you have done very well. Your article itself is good, especially considering the fact that you based your whole analysis on English poetry."

"And what, may I ask, is wrong with English poetry?" I asked, rather sharply.

"The English," he said, "are not poets. Not real poets," he insisted with conviction.

"Not real poets!" I said. "Surely you cannot have read them and say that. Shakespeare, Keats, Shelley, Wordsworth —the light that never was, on sea or land . . ."

"Precisely," he said, "the light that never was on sea or land. English poets are always in the *vagues;* they never know exactly what they are saying, or know how to say exactly what they mean. *Voilà,* the light that never was on sea or land—light that is not, that is nothing, that is nowhere. Whereas a French poet has the precise epithet for the specific thing, the unique word for the unique emotion. A French poet is an artist cutting images like marble. An English poet is a dreamer who has not learned how to speak, or to make clear what he is saying. . . . Are you feeling better now?"

As a matter of fact, I was, except for a sense of moral outrage, but I thought it not prudent to admit it quite or quite yet.

"Well, I am feeling a little better, doctor, but there's something that has disturbed my digestion."

"Look here, my friend," he said, "that will pass. I shall take care of that. But there are more important considerations than your digestion that I wish to speak of first. *Tenez,* when I was called here by the director of the hotel—a very good fellow, by the way—I was a little annoyed, for, frankly, I have much to do today. The sick have no consideration of a doctor's convenience and they have all chosen this week to be sick at once. I said to myself: 'Of course, an American tourist, who has not the equipment to, or the education to, digest our excellent French food.' I did not look forward to the prospect of seeing you. But, sir, you are a humanist, an itinerant humanist. I am a humanist, too, but, alas, my profession keeps me here in Autun where there are very few.

Now, had you arrived in this city in the Middle Ages, it would have been clear at once that you were a humanist. You would have worn a special costume; you would have spoken Latin. All the world would have known you were a humanist and you would at once have had access to the humanists of Autun—there are probably half a dozen and you shall now know them all. As it is, to whom have you spoken; to whom would you have spoken, if this wretched digestion of yours had not brought me by sheer accident to your bedside? Monsieur, there should be formed a Society of Itinerant Humanists—you and I will found it now—so that in the future when a cultivated gentleman arrives anywhere in the world he will at once be welcomed by his fellows and his peers. It will add to the interchange of ideas; it will bring kindred spirits into contact; it will prevent such as you from moving through France as if it were merely a picture book. I shall now make the usual examination, ask you the usual questions, make out the usual prescription (I think I could do it safely without the examination or the questions), and call upon you tomorrow when I expect you to be well. Then you must dine with me and, later in the week, meet one of our fellow-humanists. Do not thank me; it is in just this way that our proposed Society of Itinerant Humanists will function in the future. It is a pity that Latin is no longer the international language; *hélas,* not everyone speaks French, though they should. It is the language of the mind and, I may add, of the soul."

He asked his questions, he made his examination, he made out his prescription and hastily rose to depart. . . . I could not resist thanking him, or asking him how he came to be called Platon.

"It is the name of my father," he said brusquely and, picking up his satchel, departed.

I saw a good deal of M. Platon the next week or two. As he had predicted, in a day or two I was better; even before his examination I was already convinced that it was not ptomaine poisoning.

My third day in Autun I went to M. Platon's house to dinner. He was a widower; his small son was away at school. He lived in a house filled with massive eighteenth-century furniture, and on the walls were several nineteenth-century paintings, including one silvery early Corot. We had an excellent dinner, with a sauce for the fish which had been invented by the humanist, so Doctor Platon said, whom I should meet later in the week, and which included a touch of honey of Hymettus, for the inventor, of course, loved Greece. Remembering my recent disaster, I grew a little diffident at the succession of courses and of wines. My host observed it. He reminded me that while I might study the Stoics I was dining with an Epicurean. Over the brandy and coffee in his library he took as his theme the life of the spirit in the provinces.

"All provincial towns are alike," he said, "be they in France or America. You have read *Madame Bovary;* I have read *Main Street.* There are a few free spirits in every such town, and in France they are chiefly lawyers and physicians. There are some others: sometimes a priest, sometimes a bookseller, a librarian. In Autun there are about half a dozen, and one of them lives out in the country some ten kilometres from Autun. We must drive over to see him. He is a philologist and would like to be a novelist. During the war he served four years and carried throughout the war the Homeric hymns in his pocket. They saved him from being killed once and they kept him alive always. There is no one else in the town to talk to about the things one really cares to talk about. I go off to Paris sometimes in desperation, but I feel like a foreigner there now with so many English and Americans about, and sometimes to get as good service as a foreigner does, I pretend I am a Hollander using English as an intermediate language. It is good luck that has brought you here; perhaps I could contrive that that hotel of yours mildly poison each client who seems to be an itinerant humanist. Yet they would hardly know which to poison. The Comédie Française comes here occasionally during the summer and plays Racine in the Roman theatre. Some of the actors are cultivated people. I wrote a long poem about that theatre once."

He produced it and read a long section. It may have been better than English poetry but I had had too much food and wine to know or even completely to understand.

I took my leave. Would *monsieur le docteur* come to dine with me at the hotel? . . . I could not offer him as good a dinner, but they did very well. He would come gladly, but on one condition: frankly, he must choose his own wine. I was not stupid, but I was an American where the *vin du pays* was whisky, and where even that was forbidden.

A few days later Doctor Platon and I drove out at a wild pace to a neat, almost English-looking cottage on a wooded upland. M. Houvat, he explained, lived on a tiny income; he had been incapacitated during the war and could not carry on his university duties. He had had a novel or two published, but the philologist had got in the way of the artist. But he was a humanist in essence.

He was indeed such. It was a bright June day. We had tea and then wild strawberries, and M. Houvat, pale, slender, with one arm (the other had been lost in the trenches), talked of poetry, of Homer, and of the Homeric hymns. That was all he seemed to care to remember of the war.

"Would you like to see an amputation?" said the doctor as we drove back to town. "I must perform one now." I shuddered. "A philosopher should see everything," he said. I declined. He shrugged his shoulders.

The last night I was to be in Autun I again dined with the doctor. He had called for me to take a little stroll before going to his house. As we walked down the main street of the town he bowed almost continuously.

"You know everyone, doctor," I said. "If I walked along this street alone it would be simply a post-card view. You probably could tell me a story about everyone in this town, as you have already told me some about many of them."

"Everyone in this town is my friend, or my enemy; but they all know me. Only a nonentity remains unknown."

Toward the close of the evening, M. Platon again broached his project of the itinerant humanists. "We really should do something about it," he said. "There is only one country— it is that of people of intelligence. Its citizens are few; they should be acquainted."

I thanked my host for all his kindnesses and in the flush of the wine and the dinner said: "Doctor, I have seen a corner and an aspect of France not open to many travellers. I wonder if I might ask a favour. I have a friend who comes to Paris about once a year. He is a journalist. He meets the editors and politicians; he never leaves Paris. Might he come to Autun? Might he greet you?"

M. Platon regarded me firmly. "Your friend, you say, is a journalist? You will pardon me—I will not receive him. *Un philosophe, voilà une chose; un journaliste, c'est tout autre chose. Je regrette; je ne reçois pas votre camarade. . . . Il n'est pas humaniste itinéraire.*"

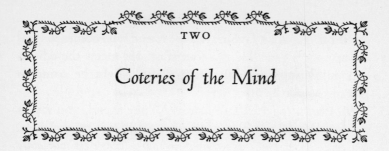

TWO

Coteries of the Mind

M. PLATON'S suggestion of a communion not of saints but of minds has much to commend it. A communion is, as a matter of fact, only a sacramental way of speaking of a *coterie*. Such a communion of minds exists in essence already and has always existed. There are humanists who are friends in the spirit although they have never met, and Platonists who see eye to eye, although they are as far apart as North Dakota and Beirut. Everyone has had the sense, on making a chance acquaintance on a steamer, at a professional meeting, in a country house, at a cocktail party (where one is likely to make a mistake), of having known that person always in essence and of two spirits' having for a long time been, unknown to each other, travelling-companions on the same road. One has the sense of having moved in parallel lines, of having touched the same beauties, shared the same truths, or nourished the same errors, found light by or aspired towards the same stars. *En route* to Italy I once met a civil engineer and in a small inn in New Hampshire, a Boston surgeon, who both quoted to me my own favourite

passages of Santayana. There are no meetings of such a society of communicants in identical objects of love, and most
of the members all their lives will never know each other.
They are simply mutually unknown communicants of the
same gods.

M. Platon's society of itinerant humanists does not exist,
and the society of stationary humanists has only a disem-
bodied Platonic being. But there do, of course, exist innumerable groups, clubs, associations, cliques, and coteries of
the interests of the spirit and the professions of the mind.
During a ceremonial opening session of the International
Congress of Religion at Brussels one September day a few
years ago, I could not help allowing my mind to wander
back over the many such I had known. For a while I maintained a kind of sociological curiosity as to what the speakers
representing each nation would say. I gathered from the very
official-sounding German delegate that religion had really
started in Germany with the advent of the National Socialist
regime. And certainly it did seem true that one religion had
then officially started. The serious study of these matters, I
gathered from the rhetorical Italian delegate (a *"filosofo con
selz,"* as they say in Italy), had begun in 1922 with the advent
of Il Duce. The French delegate was full of graciousness and
lucidity and seriousness. I regret that I cannot remember
what he said, nor do I recall that it was memorable. The
Vatican speaker brought down the house with a Latin oration; obviously the gathering felt that this was something
like the great tradition. The English speaker, a diffident Cambridge don, said he represented nobody at all except his own
university and that he felt embarrassed not to be able to speak
with authority for a whole nation, as some of the other

speakers obviously felt privileged to do. England was very negligent in these matters: it simply let people speak for themselves.

These things I gathered, but my mind at this and at succeeding sessions—especially during a very long paper on the sources of the Old Testament—wandered back over other, less distinguished associations of the mind to which I had belonged, or in which I had taken part. It was a far cry and a long time between this Congress and the first literary society I ever belonged to. It was while I was still in the seventh grade in Public School 10, Manhattan; but the club had nothing to do with the school. It was composed of a group of boys brought together by the fact that they lived in the neighbourhood and that some of them had literary interests, and that others were easily talked into joining a club, whatever the reasons for its formation or existence. I know not for what reason it was decided to call it the Benjamin Franklin Club; I think some of us had been reading Franklin's autobiography at school. I know that our chief business the first few days was to rent a small hall for the meetings, to study parliamentary procedure—some of us were great sticklers on that point—and to publish a magazine. The meetings at this late date seem, in my memory, to have been taken up largely with parliamentary procedure and with recitations. For in the period from about 1900 to 1910 everybody of good middle-class family took elocution lessons. I used to be frightfully jealous of a chum who, with a most engaging smile, would charm everyone at his parents' house Sunday evenings, reciting "Little Orphant Annie": "And the gobble-uns'll git you ef you Don't Watch Out!" Silas was a member of the Benjamin Franklin Club, but I don't think he recited those verses at any meeting. The great *tour de force* was that one of Milton Eliscu, reducing the whole club to tears one Saturday afternoon when we had a special visitors' day for the parents, "O Captain! my Captain! our fearful trip is done." It was years before I knew anything else of Walt Whitman—or, I believe, that Walt Whitman was the author of the poem—or that it was about Lincoln.

Even in those days and among us twelve-year-olds, it occurred to us, as it has increasingly occurred to older authors and publishers since, that it would be helpful and impressive to have an Introduction to the first issue of the magazine written by a distinguished man.

Living on the ground floor of the quiet apartment house in which my family lived on Morningside Avenue, below the park, was an unquestionably very distinguished-looking gentleman. He appeared every night at seven o'clock in a frock coat, with a cane, a stiff-bosomed shirt and wing collar, and enormous white moustaches. It was in the days when one knew one's neighbours in New York, and it was not a mystery to some of us why the distinguished-looking Mr. Hillis should be going to work at that hour instead of coming home as one's own father did. He was Foreign Editor of the New York *Herald*, though there seemed nothing in the least foreign-looking about him. On Sunday evenings, ever since he had made his peace with one of us whose fox terrier had bitten him, we used to be invited into the Hillises' to play dominoes. In the course of the evening we gradually learned how the news of the world poured onto Mr. Hillis's desk and how it was his enormous responsibility to decide what America should know about the European world. He was

the most important man any of us in the Benjamin Franklin
Club knew and it seemed the logical though bold step to ask
him to write the Introduction to our magazine. He wrote a
charming page, saying something to the point about the
pleasure and profit the young would get and provide by
trying their literary wings. There would be likely, he said,
to be nothing factitious in such a publication as there so often
was in the work of professional writers. It was my responsibility to read the proof. I caught the glaring error. Surely
Mr. Hillis meant "fictitious." I changed it. Only when I
proudly presented the first copy to Mr. Hillis did I find out
what factitious meant. Mr. Hillis gave me a quiet exposition
of the subject and also a somewhat stern commentary on the
importance of letting an author see proof.

The Benjamin Franklin Club did not last very long,
largely, I think, because most of the members had little
interest in literature or oratory, and the club hardly survived
the call of baseball and spring.

The second literary society to which I belonged was more
serious and devoted. It was the Webb Literary Society,
which flourished, as the phrase runs, for a number of years in
Townsend Harris Hall. It was named after a general who had
had something to do with the founding of the school. Regularly Friday afternoons we would meet and read short
stories, poems, and plays to each other. One poet used
the expression "Hell!" as an exclamation and several
fellow-writers rose to protest. "Hell is in the Bible,"
Morrie Ryskind rose excitedly to say, "and if it isn't, it's
a Hell of a Bible!" The point was thereupon regarded as
settled.

The Webb Literary Society was my introduction to conjoint and co-operative criticism. I have since then read a good deal about the function of criticism and studied many of its types and variations. One of the functions of criticism not frequently mentioned in learned analyses is the expression of a point of view just for the fun of it. Another is that of damaging the object under criticism, or the author. These particular offices of criticism were illustrated in our group. A stout and, even at sixteen, pontifical poet named Isaak Rollins used to use the period of criticism for orotund speeches on the Mission of the Poet. Others, with an early sense of authoritative standards, would show how Mr. So-and-so had failed in a story to apply the principles of narrative as outlined by Genung, and had utterly failed to remember in the Descriptive and Explanatory Parts what the principles of Exposition and Description were. These principles came out of Genung's *Rhetoric.* Some of us were certain Genung had written Burke's Speech on Conciliation, the principles of exposition in it were so clear.

The third and last of the purely literary clubs I have ever belonged to flourished at Columbia before I entered it, and has, with interruptions, flourished since—Boar's Head, deliberately misspelt as Bore's Head by the undergraduate Philistines. People wrote other things for Boar's Head besides poetry, but poetry was and is its chief *raison d'être.* And at that time John Erskine, a great teacher long before he became a bright novelist, was its centre and its power. He was, above all, a force in the classroom, especially in his course in Elizabethan literature. Even the engineering students and the football-players would go home and read Shakespeare or Dekker after he had talked about them. He was, or appeared to at least one undergraduate to be, one of those men whose essential self seemed to be tapped only, or most, in the class-room, especially at those hours—only occasional—when he seemed to have lost himself or found himself in the literature itself. I discovered or sensed for the first time the singular re-lation between love and death in listening to John Erskine lecture on *Measure for Measure*, and derived the first real sense of the Christian mystery in listening to him talk about the medieval miracle play. I was far from being the only one.

At Boar's Head, Professor Erskine was less formal, more personal, more autobiographical, and he showed many of us who had thought that poetry was an inspired wind, an ex-alted breath, that it was an art, serious, challenging, and ex-act. Some of us, including Morrie Ryskind and myself, read light verse, rather diffidently after graver themes had been broached, or the lush and tender lyrics of Hoxie Neale Fair-child or Jimmy O'Neale, baseball captain and poet, at home at once in Boar's Head and on Fraternity Row. (He was soon to die of gangrene from wounds received in action during the war.) John Erskine taught us to realize why light verse was so good a training for poetry; if it was rhythmically in-exact, or technically sloppy, it was nothing. And so some of us felt justified in writing endless verses, largely translations of Horace and Lucretius and Ennius and Propertius, with which we used to deluge Franklin P. Adams's "Conning Tower" in the *Tribune*.

Boar's Head had no magazine of its own, then, though it had had one years before and was to revive *Morningside* again later. During my senior year it conceived the grandiose pro-ject of publishing little books of verse. It got as far as one booklet, *Measures of the Moment*, by myself. They were of the Moment: the book is out of print and I have no copy myself, and the Columbia University Library's copy is missing. I cannot refrain from quoting four lines of it, the beginning of a plan I had: to translate the whole of Book II of Lucretius's *On the Nature of Things* into quatrains. I progressed as far as the first twenty lines, anyway, and I quote the first four because I believe one might render more inaccurately the temper of that grand opening in which Lucretius celebrates philosophical detachment:

> '*Tis sweet to stand upon the shore,*
> *And watch the waves in wild commotion,*
> *And to enjoy it all the more,*
> *Because you are not in the ocean. . . .*

There was one other undergraduate literary group, not a club, but an editorial board. It decided about February 1916 that something should be done to stir up the complacency of the world and of the campus. Carlton Hayes, Charles A. Beard, John Dewey, James Harvey Robinson, had been stirring up the minds of the stirrable; a war was raging in Europe and an angry pro-war wave was sweeping over the East. Energetic young college students were going off to the officers' training camps at Plattsburg and elsewhere. The *New Republic* at the time seemed to me, and to many, to be a

> *Bright elusive publication,*
> *Gospel of the social truth,*
> *Cryptic critic of the nation,*
> *Idol of the earnest youth.*

The pacifico-liberalism of the time, or what then passed for the extreme Left, needed an organ, so some of us thought. The "some" included Lincoln Schuster (it was his first publishing venture), James Marshall, now President of the

Board of Education of New York, George E. Sokolsky, who
has passed from freshman anarchism to be the apologist in
the *Herald Tribune* and *Atlantic Monthly* of things as they are.
Walter Lippmann was the philosophical voice of the liberal
movement, and James Harvey Robinson the voice of sceptical sophistication. We were taught by him in his course—
"The History of the Intellectual Classes in Western Europe"
—how much of that history was the history of pompous
human stupidity.

I don't know who thought of the title for the magazine,
but I do know where it came from. It came from a poem by
Louis Untermeyer, the title poem of one of his books which
was at the time taken seriously as the beginning of a renascence in American poetry. I have not seen the book in twenty
years and I do not imagine it is obtainable here in Sicily,
where this is being written, but it ran, I recall, something
like this:

> The quiet and courageous night,
> The keen vibration of the stars,
> Call me from morbid peace to fight
> The world's forlorn and desperate wars.
>
> The air throbs like a rolling drum,
> The brave hills and the singing sea,
> Unrest and people's faces come
> Like battle trumpets calling me.
>
> And while life's lusty banner flies
> I shall assail with raging mirth
> The scornful and untroubled skies,
> The cold complacency of earth.

It is hard to say why that particular poem should have lingered in my memory all these years. But there it is, and *Challenge* was published to assail with raging mirth almost everything, but particularly militarism. My childhood friend, Silas Seadler, formerly the expounder of "Little Orphant Annie," after a disillusioning summer at Plattsburg, wrote for us "The Menace of Plattsburg." It stirred up a good deal of dust. *Challenge* published some good poems by some good poets, including one or two already famous. It lasted two issues. I do not think its death was caused, though it may have been hastened, by a Tory satire, full principally of blank pages, published a week after our first issue and entitled *Dynamite*. That broadside was engineered by a youth later to become a mogul in Hollywood.

Tendencies on campuses, as elsewhere, come in cycles, and about ten years later, as a member of the faculty, I spoke at an undergraduate dinner of some sort. Just before the close of the evening a young man, a student in one of my classes, arose to address the gathering:

"I want to say that there is a new magazine being started to express the viewpoint of youth. We have been written about and written to; we have been exhorted; we have been explained. But this magazine is going to be written by Youth itself, which has its own viewpoint. It is free from the complacency of age, even of middle age. All those interested in writing for this youth magazine will please see me here before leaving."

"How young must one be to qualify as a writer for your publication?" I asked with a little amiable condescension as I passed.

He looked at me sternly. "Anybody who already wants to

be young is too old," he said. It was clear that a new generation was forming new coteries, and that they were not for
me and my contemporaries, however much they repeated a
pattern we too had known.

There are more fundamental and tragic symptoms, I think,
of the cycle of social and political feeling among the young.
One has on a university campus these days a depressing sense
of the *déjà vu*. I have been here before, and the time seems
to be 1916. That liberal pacifist sentiment that was for the
most part so completely transformed in a month into a passion to make the world safe for democracy has its analogue
now. Two years ago I spoke at an anti-war meeting at
Columbia; the term pacifism is less current than it was in
1916. It has come to seem to the more enterprising young of
today too supine a term and a temper. You no longer refuse
to fight; you fight fighting. Or you did two years ago. But the
young men who would twenty years ago have been writing
for *Challenge* are beginning to talk about at once fighting
war and fighting fascism, and some of them are actually already fighting in Spain. The arch-fiend was once the Kaiser;
now it is Hitler or Mussolini, or both. It would not be very
hard to promote a war sentiment in the United States, especially among the radical and idealistic young. It already seems
to many that the interests of the peace of the world lie ultimately in the preservation of the democracies of France and
England. It would not be hard to persuade the young and the
old that it is necessary to make the world safe for democracy.
It seemed necessary to many of us in 1917, who in 1916
thought war a horror we must at all costs avoid. The world
was not made safe for democracy, it appears. But this time,

we are being told, it *must* be. *Challenge* is dead, but some years ago there was started a magazine against fascism and war. It was called *Fight*.

The societies of the mind I have known since my college days have been more intransigently academic and philosophical, beginning with a club of graduate students in philosophy who met at dinner and proceeded thereafter to spend the evening discussing current technical controversies in philosophy. There is nobody quite so earnestly professional about philosophy as young and talented graduate students, nor does anything seem quite so important or ultimate as the immediately current philosophical controversies. The philosophical air of the time was full of sense and sense data, logical realisms and "ego-centric predicaments." Plato, somewhere in the *Republic,* in making his scheme for the education of the philosopher kings-to-be, counsels that dialectic be not studied by those under twenty-five. They will, he suggests, use the apparatus for empty disputation and bring all philosophy into disrepute. A student of philosophy, like a student of any other discipline, comes to respect the technique of his craft. Logic is the instrument and the asepsis of thinking, and the involvement of young minds in the professional issues is understandable and creditable. Moreover, if one sticks to the apparatus and the formulas, innocence of experience becomes less troublesome and less apparent. What we said about epistemology or logic in these dinner club meetings may have been trivial and formalistic, but it was an instinctive modesty or common sense that keeps the young, or some of them, from coming to grips with the grander problems of God, Freedom and Immortality, and the Good Life. In time, most of those who go into professional philosophy find a sense of proportion. They realize what I was early told by a distinguished teacher when I left for a year's travel and study abroad. "Remember, a professor of philosophy studies philosophy; a philosopher studies life." He failed to add that if a philosopher studies life scrupulously enough, he will have to reflect on what.it means, and he will find himself, willy nilly, studying some of the things we discussed, perhaps poorly, after very poor dinners.

Official academic meetings, philosophical associations, international congresses, and the like are graduate clubs relatively grown up. The papers read one can read later in the proceedings—those that one wants to read—but one has a chance to renew old ties, and to see the personalities and talk with the personalities out of which grew the books on one's library shelves, and occasionally to hear something whose power would not be quite the same in a book.

There are, of course, surprises. In 1930 there was an International Congress of Philosophy at Oxford. The introductory social event was a conversazione, as it was called, in the Hall of Christ Church. Everyone, with one conspicuous exception, was in evening clothes.

"Who," I asked a colleague, "is that jolly-looking little man in business clothes?" It was Benedetto Croce.

"Why don't you talk to him?" my colleague said. "You speak Italian; he apparently speaks nothing else. He looks amiable and will doubtless be glad to speak his own language. Moreover, you have long been a student of his æsthetics."

It seemed reasonable. I introduced myself and Signor Croce turned out very amiable indeed. We talked of æsthetics. I remarked that one of the reasons I was glad to have learned the Italian language was that I could now read his *Estetica* in the original. The translation was abominable.

"So I gather," he said. "But *non si deve dire*, one mustn't say so here. The translator is standing right near us."

"It does not matter," I said. "I do not believe he understands Italian."

Signor Croce smiled agreement.

Sometimes people at academic meetings look precisely as they should look, talk exactly as one would somehow want them to talk to fulfil one's expectation of them. Dean Inge, tall, gloomy, reminding one of Forbes-Robertson playing Hamlet, talking about Mysticism at a meeting of the Mind Association held at Durham one summer. Evelyn Underhill, an elderly English lady, speaking in a high treble voice and swallowing her syllables, on the same theme. S. A. Alexander, looking like a Hebrew prophet, and sounding like an English gentleman.

There are at formal meetings moments when some demon of poetry or prophecy breaks through the conventions of academic routine; when a man speaks what is in his heart or, with extraordinary clarity and cogency, what is in his head; when there is a rapier thrust in discussion or when one has the sense that one is present at the birth or the memorial of a great idea or tradition. There were the convincing words, read with great simplicity and power by Professor William P. Montague, on the function of philosophy, at the International Congress of Philosophy at Harvard in 1926; the sweep of imagination of John Dewey's closing address on the Place of Philosophy in Civilization, its provision of new perspectives of life. (The teacher's bibliographical habits persist;

that address can be found in Dewey's book of essays called *Philosophy and Civilization*.) There was the fifty-minute-long oration on Fascism by a Professor Tauro of the University of Sardinia, whose chief reason for being present was his political enthusiasm rather than his philosophical talent. There was a paper read by Sidney Hook, one freezing winter day at Amherst at the meetings of the American Philosophical Association, on "Materialism," a model of compact interpretation and clarity. There was the evening when, as a graduate student, Huh Shih, who was later to become the "Father of the Chinese Renaissance," read a paper before the Fortnightly Monday Evening Meeting of the Department of Philosophy at Columbia. It was called "The History of Chinese Logic," and I had expected it was going to be very esoteric indeed. But I was treated, as was everybody else, to something quite different. It was made clear to me for the first time how in China, at any rate, logic and morals and wisdom of life are one; and I met a Chinese humanist who explained in urbane and perfect English the meaning of the tradition of Confucius to an audience brought up on Dewey and James. I met Huh Shih last year again, on another mission. His country itself, the matrix of humanism, was now being threatened by the inhuman fascism of Westernized Japan.

But I think, of all the moments I remember at philosophical gatherings, the most memorable occurred in the Hague in the autumn of 1932 when a Congress was being held to celebrate the three hundredth anniversary of the birth of Spinoza. Various Spinozists and philosophers from all over the world were to read, not papers about Spinoza, but papers that in one way or another were in consonance with that saintly sage's approach to philosophy and religion. The first evening was devoted to an address by George Santayana. He read his essay called "Ultimate Religion." I am tempted to tell about that essay itself, in which Santayana pays his respect to nature and his adoration of those ideals which nature suggests but does not necessarily embody or realize. It was the ascetic and disciplined utterance of a liberated mind, "understanding too much to be ever imprisoned, loving too much to be ever in love." But what I remember of the occasion is not simply the paper but the temper of the reading. I had spoken often with Santayana before and had heard him pass into eloquent soliloquy. I had heard legends of the great days of his lectures at Harvard, when those who could understand understood, and those who could not were convinced by the beauty of the language and the elevation of the spirit of the man addressing them. It was the same here at the Hague. For there were many here who literally could not understand, who knew no English and certainly many—especially among the Germans and grammarians of philosophy—who, if they understood the literal words, must have found the doctrine strange and the poetry of the utterance ambiguous. But I have seldom seen an audience so rapt. Santayana read very slowly in his naturally clear and musical voice with its natural or artfully measured cadence. He read as if he were reading not simply an essay on "Ultimate Religion," but frankly, intensely, and after long brooding and reflection, his own ultimate religion. It was an act of piety to Spinoza and a confession of his own faith in which he invited all men of goodwill and honest reflection to join him. It was not a routine reading of an academic tribute. The speaker was obviously aware of the occasion and what in essence it meant. Many of the audience must have gathered it from the tone and the look of absorption in the speaker. It was clear that at least one did. For there was sitting next to me a young German, deeply absorbed. When it was over, I asked him whether he had understood. "No," he replied, "I do not understand English, but it sounded so human and so beautiful, I am sure it was." He was right.

Perhaps the true societies of the mind and those one remembers best are those that never meet, or that meet only once and by accident, or that emerge suddenly in the midst of casual conversation among a group of friends who transform it into an exchange of ideas clearly perceived and emotions directly felt, giving and catching mutual fire. And sometimes, when one is quite alone, one's imagination is peopled with ideas, those one has just been reading, those to which some reading has recently prompted one, or during or after listening to music alone. The ultimate society of the mind, when the spirit listeth, is a soliloquy, and that isolated heaven is crowded with friends in the form of congenial themes. Later, perhaps, one meets others who have in their solitude lived at some time or another in the same beatitude. I rather think that is what the great mystics, such as St. John of the Cross, meant or felt when they spoke of the loneliness of the journey toward an insight into true being and the finding of others at the end of the journey sharing the same vision. It is as if one had found one's way to a lonely mountain top by oneself on a path where one met no one, but at the peak met others who had come by their own solitary paths to the same final vista.

Instances of such chance meetings and such isolated private

peoplings of one's mind must come to everyone. I recall a few. The close of a long desultory evening in a Senior Common Room at Oxford, where I had been invited to dinner at the High Table. The conversation had been, as I found it often to be at Oxford, almost deliberately simple and casual, gossip of the county and the college, of the weather and of food. As the group included so good a talker as H. W. Garrod, the caustic and brilliant former professor of poetry at Oxford, and others not much less gifted than he, I was a little disappointed—and surprised. Over the port and nuts in the Senior Common Room after dinner, nothing much happened. There was a slow fire in the grate, but it was no slower than the conversation. Nobody said much but "Oh, really." Occasionally there was a spark in the fire. There was finally one in the conversation. Somebody mentioned something. I believe it was a church in Southern France. And then gradually, everybody throwing a little coal upon the intellectual fire, there was a blaze of light and warmth, and though God, Freedom, and Immortality were not settled by midnight, the themes had been brought out and illuminated. I cannot remember when I have heard so many people speak with such sincerity and eloquence about their ultimate convictions.

There was a luncheon party one August afternoon in Vermont, when Robert Frost began to think aloud about what was wrong with education and the young intellectuals. He was perplexed, as I had seen him before, by the way in which the mania of collectivism had seized upon people whose very temper was that of individuals and, as he thought, of individualists. The world, he said, always oscillated between Justice and Mercy. The essence of Marxism and Collectivism was mercy for all. But Nature made its own equi-

libriums, and Mercy would have to be balanced by Justice.
I am not sure Frost made it quite clear that justice, as he conceived it, was anything very much more than a survival of
the fittest. But it was clear that he thought that, too, was a
kind of justice, and that much of the feeling against war and
against poverty was unwholesome sentimentalism. The poor
we should not only always have with us, but poverty bred
an indomitableness and strength, and the only revolutions
that were worth having or that were effective were those
that were paid for in blood. He had been accused, he said, of
being a counter-revolutionary, but at least he was not a
bargain counter-revolutionary making his revolutions in
words. There were some of us present, including one who
was very young and very Marxist, who quarrelled with
Frost. But the same poet was speaking here who had spoken
in "something there is that doesn't love a wall," and one
could disagree with this poet but one could not quarrel with
him. To quarrel with a genuine poet's taste was like quarrelling with the colour of a child's eyes. And it was the eyes
of a candid—and stubborn—New England child that were
looking out upon the tides of our world.

There was an evening (it had been very gay) when a group
of people, including a very modernist composer and a pian-
ist, were gathered in the same room on the same mountain-
side. There had hardly been a serious word all evening.
Somebody suggested we play a little music, and put on a
phonograph the slow movement of the first *Brandenburg
Concerto* of Bach. It had that poignancy and depth of feeling
that still the mouths of those who treat Bach as if he were
simply a highly skilled musical mathematician. Everyone
was stilled, even by the second-rate representation on a port-

able phonograph. There ensued a controversy as intense as if one's ultimate moral convictions were being tested—as perhaps they were—on what were really the unquestionably great moments in music; where and what composers had written passages that had the note of ultimacy and the cadence of absolute musical and imaginative power. The Wagner, anti-Wagner battle broke out again, and there was a pitched battle between those who found Wagner the great rhetorician and those who held him the soaring and impassioned spirit of the love duet of *Tristan,* or of the outburst of sheer musical gladness as in the great quintet of the third act of the *Meistersinger*. The battle broke out over Debussy; whether he was a skilful and esoteric trifler or whether, as some of us thought, there was a note of exquisite pathos and distance and nuance of spirit in him that was unique in musical history. A war was raging in Spain and another one in China, and another might soon be raging in all Europe; and yet even those whom such a haunting nightmare of contemporary disaster preoccupied had forgotten it. When the ultimate questions of human equity shall have been settled, the passions of men may be absorbed by ultimate questions of taste. The arts are the languages of men, and a passionate conflict over a symbol may be as symptomatic as the quarrel over a religious and political creed. But in such matters quarrels become discussions, and the discussions are innocent. Our quarrel over taste divided but educated rather than destroyed us. The same is hardly true of the quarrels of men over politics and morals. The only peaceful societies are the societies of the mind, for in such societies alone, one gains by sharing, and communication is contagion and growth.

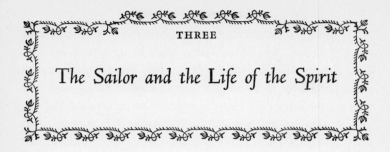

THREE

The Sailor and the Life of the Spirit

Occasionally one writes something that seems to a few readers in far places to be addressed directly to them, to speak specifically of them, and they are moved to write to the author as to an unknown friend. In 1926 I published an imaginary portrait called *Richard Kane Looks at Life*. It was an attempt to give a picture of the awakening mind of the more sensitive American college student. I mention it here because, had I not published it, I should never have come to know Jewell V. Jones, able seaman, and I should not be writing of him now.

I had received a whole sheaf of letters from young men and women just in college or just out of it or ten years after their degree. How did I know? I had written their autobiography. It was gratifying, of course, to believe that without realizing it I had written the pattern of the spiritual problems of young women in South Carolina and young men in California, in both of which places I had never been. The letters followed, on the whole, identical patterns, and I became anæsthetized to them. But there came in the mail one morning a communication that arrested my attention, first by the address at its head, and secondly by the unexpected background of the writer, and by a certain curiosity-provoking élan in the writing. If I had known I was some day going to write my recollections I might have kept it. But the force of necessity—near-sightedness—has blessed me, *per forza,* as the Italians say, with a good memory, and I believe the letter ran substantially as follows:

Brooklyn Navy Yard,
Dec. 5, 1926.

Dear Sir,

I am a gob in the United States Navy, twenty-six years old. I have been in the Navy four years and I have just re-enlisted. Before enlisting for the first time, I had bummed around the country on various odd jobs, trucking, dish-washing, etc. I was one of seven children in a white trash family in the mountains of Kentucky. So you see the accidents of my life are not Richard Kane's, but in essence you have written my autobiography.

The letter continued to say that Mencken might shout and Will Durant might bawl (the *Story of Philosophy* was then all the rage), John Erskine might smile his deep, knowing smile about life (*The Private Life of Helen of Troy* had appeared the year before), but there were certain things I had done that were unparalleled in American literature. Among others I was clearly "America's master of alliteration."

The source, the tone, the strange medley of directness and rhetoric, of insight and naïveté, prompted me to wonder about Jewell V. Jones. I think I was especially taken by the philosophical sentence about essence and accidents. How did that get into the vocabulary of a gob with such a history? I looked at the address again. Brooklyn Navy Yard. Perhaps the U.S.S. *Detroit* was still in port. I wrote a note to Jewell V. Jones inviting him to come to see me. The letter had said, apparently wistfully, that he had never had any personal relations with a writer in his life.

A few days later I received the following reply:

Three days ago I wrote you a sincerely appreciative letter. In return I received a two-page typewritten outline, headed "Experience and Metaphysics." It was unsigned. But I can think of nobody except you who would conceivably write to me who would be interested in such matters. Is this an oracular and mystical way of giving me advice, or is it simply a piece of professorial absentmindedness?

I had already discovered my mistake the evening before at Cooper Union, where I had taken out of my portfolio not the notes I meant to have brought with me, but a note to Jewell V. Jones. It had not been fatal. One sometimes gives a better lecture for having forgotten one's notes. The letter killeth. I tried again. I wrote again asking Mr. Jones if he would telephone me and let me know whether he could come to dinner with me, and when. The next evening about ten-thirty the telephone rang. He was sorry to telephone so late but he had just got off the boat. He had asked the operator to "ring softly" lest I be already asleep. It was a soft Southern drawl that came over the wire.

"You really don't want to see me, sir. I should only bore you. I have nothing to say. I'd like to listen, but I'm afraid you're much too busy."

I insisted.

Promptly the next evening, at seven to the dot per appointment, there was a vigorous ring at the doorbell of my apartment. I opened the door to see standing before me in a gob's uniform a powerfully built young man, six foot three at least, with a gentle expression and, I could not help observing, a pair of strong, enormously large hands, one of which firmly gripped mine. Mr. Jones came in diffidently.

"I could not make up my mind whether or not you'd be embarrassed by my coming in my uniform," he drawled hesitantly. "I know what people think of sailors."

"How absurd, Mr. Jones!" I said. "It's late and perhaps you are hungry; let's go over to the Faculty Club, which is close by, and talk at dinner."

"Oh, no," he said with a look of genuine alarm, "then they'll *surely* think you're the most idiosyncratic professor at Columbia."

"I don't like the 'surely,'" I said.

But Mr. Jones was firm. He would not imperil an academic reputation by coming to the Faculty Club in sailor's uniform as my guest. We went to a restaurant in the neighbourhood and returned to the apartment after dinner. Jewell V. Jones told me a good deal about his education, which was largely of his own making, and of his reasons, quite considered, for going into the Navy and staying there. Ever since he could remember he had been interested vaguely in philosophical questions. What it was all about, what one could believe, what one meant by time and by the good life. He had knocked about the country for years, and nothing seemed to come of his life. He had no particular ambitions, save that of understanding existence and making a contemplative peace with it. It had dawned on him that the Navy would be just the thing. If it had been the Middle Ages, he said, he would have gone into a monastery. American life was full of hasty ambition; it led nowhere when successful, and he doubted that he would have been successful. The Navy was the perfect thing for him. He was in the Signal Corps where they had plenty of leisure, and a light to read by. He could read hours at a stretch and could have the spaces of the long days at sea for thinking. He had thought about a lot of things: God, freedom, immortality, and, well, the state of the world.

"Do you have much trouble getting books?" I asked.

"That's just the trouble," he said. "I can't buy many, and I don't quite know what to buy. But I subscribe to all the —what do they call them?—quality magazines: the *Atlantic*, the *Century*, *Scribner's*, the *Nation*, etc. I read *Richard Kane* when it came out in the *Century*. I lent it to the captain. And when I am in New York there's a fair library at the Soldiers' and Sailors' Club, and of course I go to the New York Public Library at Forty-Second Street."

"But you must want people to talk to about the things that seem to interest you," I said. "Surely you don't find many contemplative philosophers on board the cruiser *Detroit*."

"No, I don't; but I get along well with my shipmates. I'm young, too, you know, and we're all full of animal spirits. They're nice chaps. Most of them are in the Navy because they couldn't stand being at home any more. Many of them have stepmothers."

"Do any of your companions know about these intellectual interests of yours?" I asked. "Don't some of them regard them as a little queer?"

"Oh, they notice I read a lot, and they think it's some kind of deep stuff. They sometimes tease me about it. They call me the Professor."

"I don't suppose they ever ask you about such things, do they?"

"Oh, once in a while. You know a group of men, if they talk long enough, hit upon what you call somewhere Ultimate Things. I heard some of them discussing the belief in a future life one day, and one of them said: 'Ask Jones; he knows.' "

"You know as much about that as most authorities on the subject," I suggested.

At half-past nine a friend of mine dropped in unexpectedly. He had been an officer in the Navy during the war. Jones and he talked shop a little. Suddenly, to my friend's amusement and to my embarrassment, the sailor turned to my friend and, leaning forward, said:

"Mr. Burrill, don't you think Mr. Edman writes well?"

My friend said, smiling, that he thought I did, sometimes.

"But I mean," persisted Mr. Jones, "don't you like his lyric flights?"

"When they're controlled flights," was the reply. My visitor had only the day before pointed out a page in which I had, as he put it, "gone roller skating on the rainbow."

"Controlled flights," said Sailor Jones with impatience, and rose and spat on the floor. There are all stages of definitiveness in criticism. Jones was more forthright than most reviewers.

The talk drifted to music, and I played some, a new record of Mozart's Minuet from *Don Giovanni*. The sailor listened attentively. "I wish I could hear more music," he said.

As he was leaving that evening, he said: "This is the first time in my life I have spoken to a person who really lives with the things I am interested in. I am very grateful. But I am going to ask a favour. You know you asked me before, whom I can talk to about the things that I like to think about. Well, there is really no one. I have a girl friend in Florida; she's a stenographer. I put a lot into letters to her that I am not sure she cares much to read. Just to get it out of my system. Might I write to you occasionally? I know you're busy and won't have time to answer, and I know my letters will sound simple-minded. But it would help me to get it out of my system onto paper. Do you mind? You needn't answer; my letters will be frequent and they'll be long."

"I should be delighted," I said, "and I shall answer as often as I can. And you must come to see me whenever you are in port."

"It won't be often," he said; "we're off next week for manœuvres in the Pacific; you know, you've been reading about it in the papers, in the interest of peace."

From then on, from time to time, I would get long letters from Jewell, single-spaced, typewritten, full of his comments on everything he had been thinking and reading about. They were strange blends of perception and simple-mindedness. He had all the faults of the self-educated man as well as his virtues. There would be *bravura* phrases followed by grammatical mistakes, and a ruthless devastation of Eddington or Jeans followed by a piece of sentimental mysticism or innocence. "I read your article on Spinoza in the Sunday *Times*," he wrote once; "I have sent it to my girl friend in Florida." Or, again: "We have arrived in Oporto after a week's simulated naval warfare at sea. I found my February *Atlantic* awaiting me. In it concludes Mr. Joseph Wood Krutch's *The Modern Temper*. The editor of the *Atlantic* remarks it is now an open season for Joseph Wood Krutch. Well, I shall begin. I think Mr. Krutch's pessimism is just a form of masochism thinly disguised. I wish somebody would remind him that the question, 'Is life worth living?', as Samuel Butler puts it, is a question fit for an embryo, not for a man." There would be disquisitions on what was wrong with sea writers and why he didn't propose to become one. There would be inquiries as to how a naturalistic philosophy (such as I had recently outlined in the *Nation* under the title of "The New Naturalism") could ever give a comprehensive meaning to life in the way that the older theologies or metaphysical idealisms did. There would be Whitmanesque pæans, though he did not like Whitman, on the self-justification of being young and healthy and content in the sun.

It was some months before I saw my sailor friend again. He had telephoned that he was in New York and I had invited him to Sunday dinner at one. It was one-thirty when he came rushing in, browned, hatless, coatless, flurried, and a large package under his arm.

"I'm sorry to be late," he said. He handed me the package. "This is for you. I forgot it at the Soldiers' and Sailors' Club and I was afraid I'd be late, so I took a taxi back there and up here. Well, I'm pretty late anyhow."

"You shouldn't spend money like this on me," I said.

"You know us sailors; when we're in town we spend money wildly, and I choose to spend it like this. It's my own funeral."

He had brought the Beethoven *Third Symphony*. I was touched and embarrassed.

"Have you ever," I said with a sudden idea, "been to a symphony concert?"

"Never," he said.

"Will you come with me this afternoon—I have two tickets—unless you have other plans?"

"We each have a complex," he said. "Mine is that my uniform embarrasses you; yours is that I'd rather be somewhere else when I'm here."

Jewell was quite excited by the sight of the orchestra (he was surprised to find it actually on the stage); he looked a little self-conscious when I introduced him to a friend in the row in front of us. He settled down with the most complete attention when the orchestra launched into the singing theme that begins Brahms's *Third Symphony*. I quite forgot my guest during the music. There is nothing so engulfing as waves of orchestral sound when one is in the mood and the orchestra is in the vein. And there were certain things, besides, I was watching for in the score. I wanted to be sure not to miss that final ingenious quietude in which, high on the violins, Brahms repeats at the end of the fourth movement what he had sung full-throatedly on at the beginning.

During the intermission Jewell said very little, except to remark that he had not known that there could be so much and such rich sound in the world.

The second half of the programme consisted of excerpts from Wagner, the usual things: The Ride of the Valkyries, the Siegfried Rhine Journey, the Prelude to the *Meistersinger*. The sound of the old war horses galloping on a Sunday after-

noon did not promise too much, and I was in any case tired
musically from having tried to listen to everything that was
going on in the Brahms. My attention wandered every now
and then to Sailor Jones. He certainly had no attention for
me. He sat forward listening as if there were no other world
and no other being save those poignant violins and impera-
tive trombones, and with the climax of the *Meistersinger* he
could scarcely contain himself.

"Boy!" he said when he had finally stopped applauding,
"that Wagner certainly could whoop it up. What a man! Do
you think we could get him to play it again?"

I said it was extremely unlikely.

"Come and have the sailor's delight with me," Jewell said
as we walked out, "coffee and a ham sandwich."

We went to a near-by cafeteria. It was a mild day, pre-
scient of spring. Jewell was lost in reflection. After he had
finished his coffee in silence, he lit a cigarette, and smoked on
without a word.

"How did you like the concert?" I said to him. Except for
the exclamation about Wagner, he had said not a word
about it.

"Well, frankly, I didn't get much out of the Brahms; that
went over my head. But the Wagner didn't" (he pronounced
the name as if it were English); "that had all the obviousness
of ecstasy." And then with no apparent connexion he asked
suddenly: "Do you ever read the Gospel of St. John?"

"Sometimes."

"Remember what he says about the Word become Flesh?
It's a wonderful phrase and it tells a lot about writing. The
Word become Flesh. Some writing is that. Touched with

flame, certain writing is. The spirit become incarnate. You can tell at once the real thing from the fake. That Wagner music has it: touched with flame. And if a writer doesn't have it, I can't read him very much. Will you have another cup of coffee?"

"You don't propose to stay in the Navy all your life, Jewell?" I said when he turned up once a few months later and had been talking as usual about books and ideas.

"Well, I'm in it for the present. Then I don't know. Don't tell me I ought to write. I know I wouldn't have enough to say and I really wouldn't know how to say it very well. It's different just writing letters. I really am happy in the Navy, though everybody tells me to get out of it. There's an old lady who comes down to give us coffee and cake at the Soldiers' and Sailors' Club. She talked with me for a while and said: 'But why are you in the Navy? You should be writing or studying.' 'Ma'am,' I said, 'just let me stay in the Navy. It's a good place to be one's self; that's awfully hard on land.' I've tried to think of what job I could find on land, and I think I've thought of one. When my term in the Navy expires, I'm going to become a Borden's milkman, right here in New York, if I can."

"But why a milkman?"

"It would give me my days free, and I would have a chance to read in the libraries and it'd keep me out of the distractions. Of course, I don't know how my girl friend— she's a stenographer in Florida now—will like it. You know we're going to be married one of these days."

"Is she interested in the contemplative life?" I asked.

"No, but she's learning, and I've told her a lot, and she's glad that I am."

I did not hear from Jewell for quite a long time. He finally wrote me that he had decided that it wasn't fair taking up my time when he came to town; he had nothing to offer and it was no use pretending: the chasm between those who had really been educated and those who hadn't was too profound. I had been very kind and he would remember me always, but I had enough to do, and hadn't too much energy. He wished he could lend me some of his vitality; perhaps I wouldn't always be having the colds I seemed to have whenever he turned up in New York.

I wrote him a letter explaining there was only one community and that was of the mind, and we were both members of it. He came again when he was in port.

About a year later, faithful Maria, who takes care of my apartment, told me a milkman, not the regular one but one she had never seen before, wished to see me. It was Jewell. He looked odd in his milkman's cap and white jacket, but the same healthy being as before.

"I've got the job," he said.

"I'm delighted to see you again," I said. "And how's the life of the spirit on shore?"

"Fair," he said, "but there are distractions, pleasant ones. I'm married now to the girl friend in Florida."

Jewell has been married some years now. There is a little boy who bears the writer's name. Jewell seems happy, though less exuberantly than of old, and he finds it difficult, he tells me when I see him, to keep up with ideas now. "And philosophical ideas don't seem such cures for the world as I used to think," he said, "not the world I see around me on shore and read about in the papers."

I gathered that on a milkman's wages and with a wife to support and a child to bring up, things in general are not touched with flame, nor is ecstasy as obvious any more.

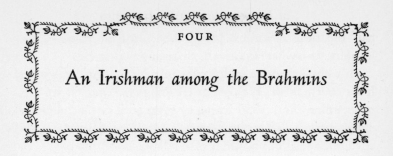

FOUR

An Irishman among the Brahmins

ONE meets originals among the students every year at a university; some years one of them stands out so that years later that year seems academically to be memorable, or to be earmarked as his. The first I heard of young George O'Connor was a telephone call from the Dean of the College. He was, the Dean said, either a lunatic or a genius, perhaps a little of both. In any case, he thought I had an appreciation of both categories and would find O'Connor interesting. He had had a scrambled education, partly abroad, and had a disordered but vivid mind. Perhaps I could advise him a little. The Dean added that he thought that O'Connor and I would have much in common.

I had hardly put down the telephone when there was a vigorous knock on my door and there entered a young man, powerfully built, with a fresh, rosy face and a head of wild, wavy brown hair. He waved a college catalogue at me.

"My name's O'Connor," he said. "The Dean said you could help me, maybe. I can't find my way through this catalogue, and I don't know what in it to believe, or what half the time it means. Now, this course of yours—Philosophy 72—what on earth is that supposed to be?"

"It's quite clear," I said, rather primly, "in the catalogue. It's a course in the Philosophy of Religion in which we try to examine the typical forms of religion and the religious experience, the relation of theology to the religious experience, the social implications of religion; it's all there."

"Is it worth taking?" he asked, looking at me with his lively blue eyes. There was not a trace of impertinence in his question; he asked simply for information.

"That's a little hard for me to say," I said. "I believe it is, of course, but you would have to be the judge. The subject is unquestionably interesting and important. . . ."

"I know," he said, studying the catalogue carefully. "But these catalogue descriptions aren't worth very much. I've found that out. They all sound so grand. It depends a lot on the man. Students here speak well of it, but students speak well of courses for such accidental reasons. Everyone says it's bright and entertaining. But, well, you know what I mean. Is it worth *taking?* Does it really give you new ideas, or do something to your old ones? Does it make you over, or give you a new world?"

"You want a religious revelation," I said. "This is a course —a course in the philosophy of religion; it is not a religion, or a revelation; it is not intended to be."

"But that's the trouble. I want to know if it's just another course."

"You might try it," I said. "You can always drop it after a week."

George did try it, and tried a seminar besides. In the

course, since it was a lecture course, he could not say very
much, but he would break in in the afternoon with a blazingly new—or what seemed to him a blazingly new—idea
he had come upon, in Eddington, in Whitehead, in himself;
or sometimes one that he alleged he had got from me. In the
seminar, on Plato, he would say things that he had picked
up from Heaven knows where. They were not always to the
point, but they never failed to have one of their own. I came
to know something about him. His father had made a fortune in the lumber business in the West, and had taken his
whole family to Europe, much as Henry James, Sr., had
taken his family, on the ground that there were no satisfac-
tory schools in America. And, apparently, his father had not
been satisfied with those in Europe either. For the family had
gone from place to place for several years; George had been
in a progressive school in Germany (it was before the days
of Hitler), to a strict Calvinist school in Geneva, to another
progressive school in England; at the age of sixteen he had
become the junior friend of the group of expatriate writers
in Paris. He spoke familiarly, justly so, of Ernest Heming-
way, and had, I think, been to Spain with him.

He found the chains of a regular academic routine galling.
The whole apparatus of examinations, of books to be read
at given times, of classes at regular hours—all seemed to him
inordinately silly. When he read, he read with perspicacity
and accuracy, but he could not be trusted to read a book
when assigned. I tried to win him to a sense of the necessary
discipline of the intellectual life, especially for a young man
who wished to be a writer. "You must know something to
write about," I said, "and you must be clear. You can learn
a lot here and a lot about handling what you learn."

George seemed to agree. For a few weeks there would be work and there would be a diminution of protest. But one day, along about the middle of November, George appeared looking very grave.

"I am leaving college," he said. "I can't stand it any more. I don't see how you can."

"What's the matter," I asked, *"now?"*

"Just the same as always," he said, intensely; "the place is too confoundedly intellectual. All the intellectual words, but no ideas with life in them. Ghosts of the mind walking around the campus. I often wonder how you can stand it, but I caught sight of you crossing the campus the other day, and I began to understand why. You're absorbed and you're near-sighted. You don't see that it's there."

He took out a typewritten manuscript, single-spaced, and apparently long. "Would you look at this?" he said. "It's a resignation I am sending, with explanations, to the Dean."

It was indeed a resignation with explanations! With citations from everybody from Rousseau to Dewey, George explained to the Dean that, despite the many kindnesses of the latter, and all the concessions he had made him, he must leave college. Education, George explained, was in a bad way, and it was doing everything it could to kill the souls of its students and paralyse their minds. It gave all the vocabulary of ideas, but few ideas, and those ideas were dead. It substituted method for substance; it was the shell and husk of intellectual training and imaginative life. George could put up with it no longer. He was leaving. That, with all the rhetoric—or most of it—boiled away, was what George had to say to the Dean. It was a sort of manifesto; George felt that by leaving college he had nothing to lose but his chains, the irons that were constricting his spirit.

"Shall I send it?" he said.

"I think not," I said. "It's pretty theatrical, a little impolite and unappreciative, and it's unjust. Half the things you say here you learned here. You have built up a monster simply for the sake of destroying it. If you'd spent more time on your courses and less on your sensitive soul, you'd get further and be wiser. May I tear up the letter? You've got it out of your system."

George smiled amused, half-reluctant agreement. I tore the letter into pieces and threw them into the waste-basket. I wish now I hadn't done so. Some of it would be worth quoting now, for it was, for all its bravura, far from silly. George was, it is true, ingeniously finding reasons for not doing the work he was supposed to be doing for his courses. He would have read Malinowski's work on primitive religion if he had found it on his own; but it became a tyranny of the academy when it was prescribed, as it was, for the course he was taking with me. But I knew many of the things he said were sound, and what was more, he knew that I knew it. He was an incarnation, not unengaging, of the eternal malcontent on a campus, the perpetual, surprised discoverer of the way in which the machinery of a university, like the machinery of many other enterprises, defeats its purposes by swallowing them. So had many a mystic in the Church of which George was still a communicant rebelled against the ecclesiastical organization. Thus had many a pietist in eighteenth-century Germany rebelled against the intellectualism of those who spent their lives proving and defining the God whose being they no longer felt and whose presence they had long forgotten. There must be many, among both students and teachers, who have come to feel as George now felt. But among the teachers the machinery had itself often become engrossing, and there were students to whom the machinery and the formulas were all education meant, or could mean. I had seen two or three of the liveliest minds and most imaginative tempers among students who had fled from, or been exiled from, the academy because they had felt as George now felt, and adapted themselves less than he. And I had also seen what had in time become of some of them. It requires a very strong character, tenacity of purpose, and singleness of aim to work in isolation, especially when one is young. Liveliness of mind and acuteness of feeling often disintegrate into nothingness without the discipline of a period of orientation in principles, in intellectual handling of facts; the discovery of the manner in which facts themselves are distinguished from fancies, the way in which facts themselves are discovered. I tried to explain some of this to George, and to point out that the thirst for experience is slaked but not satisfied if one has not the equipment through which experience becomes enriched with meaning. That was, on the whole, what an intellectual training could do for a poet or a mind. It could do it despite the mechanization of a university, the routine of the classroom, the formal habit of mind inevitable among those who repeatedly deal with the same materials which they expound year after year to the uninformed and, for the most part, uncritical young.

"You sound fair enough," George said. "I'll be good; I'll try again, and I promise not to come in with a manifesto or a resignation for a couple of months, anyway."

"Good," I said.

"Yes, I know," he continued, "people in this university are too busy to be bothered by the raising of fundamental issues."

"Not only in universities, George."

"I'll be good," said George. "I see you have quiz books to read."

He was "good," too, for quite a long period. He did remarkably well on the examinations at mid-term, including those in courses that he did not like or value very highly. I was rather pleased with the conversion I had made. I looked forward to a sobered George who should combine the vitality and freshness of a poet's temper with the discipline of a scientist's method and a philosopher's analysis. Something would come of that youth yet. There was a lot to be said for the collegiate apparatus when tinctured with sympathy and understanding; so I congratulated myself.

I was a little premature. It was April. The sunlight played softly over streets that made one long to be where there were no streets at all. George was not the only one in that afternoon class whose mind and eyes seemed to be elsewhere. I had a hard time myself keeping to the theme of the relation between religion and science. I returned to my office and sat wondering. "Great God! I'd rather be a pagan suckled in a creed outworn." I wondered why the solar system was so arranged, or the Gregorian calendar, that Easter vacation came so late this year. It would be pleasant to stand on a lea and have glimpses that might make one less forlorn.

There was a knock on the door; George appeared and began decisively and without preliminary:

"I haven't come this time to ask you whether you think I *ought* to leave college. I am leaving. That is settled. I'm going to Bermuda and I don't know how long I shall stay. But I know I am not coming back to the university. It's no go. Perhaps it's my fault, but there's something wrong with this college. It isn't all my fault. I'm not the only one. Oh, I know: you'll tell me I'd stay if I had to; that I'm a spoilt child of the rich; that I'm self-indulgent and romantic; that I lack discipline. You've told me all that before. . . . Some of it is true. But this time I've made up my mind. And I've made up my mind about something else, too. I think *you* ought to come along. . . ."

"But the term isn't over, George. I can't just pack up and leave and go to Bermuda, even if I wanted to. As a matter of fact, I do."

"But why not?" said George. "You will have to leave some time. April is as good a time as any to quit this death in life. I've been thinking about you. It's rather remarkable that you've kept alive at all; it really is. Committee meetings, papers, quizzes, professional meetings, the same courses year after year. I've come to tell you, if you will permit the impertinence, that it is still possible to save your soul. If you don't come now, once and for all, you probably never will. I'm sailing on Friday; that gives you three days. I shall come in tomorrow to ask you what you've decided."

George was quite impatient with me the next day when he returned and found me still unprepared to go out into the Indian wilderness, first stop Bermuda, and abandon the educational market-place. He almost pleaded with me not to commit myself irrevocably to the sterility of the society of teachers and scholars. He went to Bermuda and I received a note from him. He was bicycling and reading Wordsworth's *Prelude.*

I haven't heard from George save indirectly since. He's given me, as well as the university, up as a job. That was ten years ago. But the fact that, so far as I can gather, in point of fame or worldly success George has not amounted to very much does not prove that he was altogether wrong or that morally or spiritually he is a failure. Oxford and Shelley had a difficult time with each other, too. I do not think the university would have destroyed George; it might have made him. But I have seen spirits destroyed; youthful lovers of literature turned into pedants, some of them now quite respected in academic circles; lovers of wisdom petrified into classroom exponents of doctrine; passionate revolutionaries turned into reactionaries, or, perhaps even more sadly, passionless liberals. I have seen the word become deadened by the flesh, and the letter kill the spirit. And on April days sometimes still I feel a trip to Bermuda or somewhere, and for ever, might be good for some of us in the academy and for the academy itself. The mystics and the heretics are important events in the history of the Church of a living God. Saints have flourished in solitude and visions have been seen there.

But George was mistaken in thinking the greatest stultification comes in the academy; one sees it worse outside. The students I knew best at college are shocking to meet sometimes ten years after. They were awakened at and by college, by ideas and imagination. The world, not the academy, killed them, and George by this time must be complaining about the world on the same grounds upon which he used to cavil at the college. For the greatest regimentations come not from ideas, nor from the machinery of academic life, but from the machinery of living. Or George may have found out, on the other hand, how empty freedom can be.

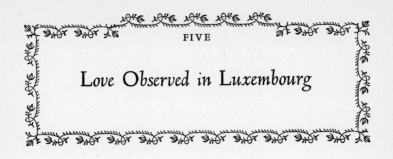

FIVE

Love Observed in Luxembourg

THE advantages of being alone in travelling are not to be despised. Alone one leaves one's world behind, and if one needs or enjoys human relationships, one must adapt oneself to human beings in *their* setting, not in one's own, and discover, not altogether unpleasantly, that there is no place like home. People are cordial to *one* stranger who would be diffident with two. And occasionally I have found that, when they discover one is a foreigner, a teacher, and a bachelor, they will confide their problems or private feelings as they would not to anyone more involved in the life of their town or of their friends, or in life itself. I am quite sure, had I come to Luxembourg accompanied, or had Mlle. Nikels, the director of the little inn at Clairvaux, not classified me as quite out of her world, and almost out of any world, she would not have told me the two main problems of her life: her father and a young man who . . .

As a matter of fact I should not have known Mlle. Nikels or the Duchy of Luxembourg if it had not been that a Frenchman had convinced me that Switzerland was dull.

"I leave tomorrow," I had said to the young French doctor in Paris, "for Switzerland."

"Why Switzerland?" he said.

"I hate Paris in the summer; it's already June and I want to get off to a quiet place to read and write."

"But Switzerland is banal—*tout à fait banale*," he said.

I reflected on the picture-postcard views, the English on holiday, the standard hotel meals, the quiet orderliness in which one wished sometimes one might hear a pistol shot, the endless milk-chocolate shops and jewellery shops, the yodelling, the funiculars, the almost German slowness of Swiss French, and the unintelligibility of Swiss German. I was given pause.

"But where *should* one go?" I said, sighing.

"Luxembourg," he said promptly and definitively, "Luxembourg!"

"And why Luxembourg?" I asked. It had never occurred to me. I had not thought of it since the news of the Germans' passing through it had been in the headlines when I was a sophomore.

"Because Luxembourg is divine," he said, his eyes lighting. "I spent a most wonderful vacation there a year or two ago. It is a cameo, a miniature. It is a little country and everything in it is little: the inns, the mountains, the waiters, the people, the prices. It is divine!"

Obviously, it must have its points. I began to be interested. "Do you know any place to go in Luxembourg?" I asked.

"I am not sure I remember the name, but I believe the village is called Clairvaux. It is about sixty miles from the capital city, Luxembourg. There is a small inn; it used to be a private villa, I believe. Clairvaux is a very small place but everyone will know it. You should go. Luxembourg is divine."

"How does one get a passport for Luxembourg?" I asked. He did not remember. Nobody in Paris seemed to know. The Luxembourg consul was not in the telephone directory. I finally ascertained that he had office hours on Thursdays and Saturdays between one-thirty and two-thirty in his private residence. The hours, too, were diminutive. The next day was Thursday. The Luxembourg consul seemed a little surprised by a visit from somebody who had no particular business in the Duchy. Only Belgians visited it, he said, and then not before July.

The following afternoon I arrived in the city of Luxembourg, in which (perhaps I saw with the eyes of my French friend) everything did seem diminutive, and the castle on one side of the river reminded me of something long ago. I suddenly remembered: it was *The Count of Luxembourg,* a musical comedy of about 1912 which for some obscure reason I had as a child not been allowed to see. By noon the next day I found myself in a small village with another castle overlooking it, and nestled among small-scale mountains. I identified the hotel, about half a mile out of town. It was a white house with a pleasant garden and a small landscaped park. It looked scarcely like an inn at all. As I entered I found myself in what seemed a combination lounge and village café—I found later it had been the entrance hall. A tiny elderly middle-aged man came to greet me in what sounded like Alsatian German. I was shown to a large, spotless, high-ceilinged, white-walled bedroom overlooking the little park. From my window I could see the castle and the village nestling below it, and the hills. I felt I should be very comfort-

able here indeed. And I had seen from the train a rolling landscape, half woodland, half meadow, that had looked most
inviting for walking or bicycling. The rates were tiny, too.
I wondered what the food would be like. After dinner I
wondered how it came to be so extraordinarily good. The
potage and the *poulet chasseur* were such as one found in famous Paris restaurants.

I walked into the café after dinner. There was a small
group, some of them playing skat at a corner table, apparently habitués. The café was presided over by a short, brisk,
intelligent young woman, friendly but plain, who turned
out to be the innkeeper's daughter. Everybody was speaking
in a dialect I could not very well understand, I judged Alsatian. The innkeeper himself, an extremely short man, was
sitting by the skat-players, not playing, but apparently giving advice about the game and discourse about things in
general. He eventually deserted the players and came over to
ask me whether I was comfortable, and whether there was
anything I desired. He spoke German but used, in the course
of it, two or three French expressions.

"*Vous parlez français, alors?*" I said. "I thought German
was the language here."

M. Nikels regarded me with horror. He drew himself up
to all of his short height and said: "Monsieur, there was a
time when we spoke German here because we had to. But
our native language is Luxembourgeois, quite different, and
our culture is entirely French. No one goes from here to
Berlin; one goes from here to Paris, and not only because
the distance is shorter. Our modes, our books, our ideas are
all French. It is a relief to me that you speak the language."

From then on M. Nikels and I, Mlle. Nikels and I, spoke

only French, and it was the language I used also with M. Felens, the dentist, M. Delens, the advocate, and M. Tonens, the doctor, who gathered each night in the café to play skat and discuss local and world affairs. For the café of the Hôtel du Parc was the café of the higher bourgeoisie of the village; the only workingmen I ever saw there were the two who came in on a truck twice a week to deliver the beer and remain long enough to consume some of it.

I found the Hôtel du Parc a delightful quiet place to work in. After a morning's writing or reading I would descend to the bar, have a vermouth, and pick up gradually a good deal about the origin and nature of the family and the establishment in which I found myself. The mystery of the almost pretentiously good food in so small and unpretentious an inn was soon cleared up.

"How comes it, M. Nikels," I asked, "that you have so elegant and *soignée* a *cuisine?* It is not only that it is good but it has the hand of one of the grand masters of the art. Who is the cook? I thought I had a glimpse of him once and he seemed very young."

"He is. He is my son; he is twenty years old."

"But where did he learn to cook so well?" I asked.

"From the great masters of the art at Paris," he said, proudly. "He made his higher culinary studies there. You understand, monsieur, I am not a *hôtelier* by profession. I am a horticulturist. My wife, whom you have not seen, still directs our horticultural establishment at the town of Diekirch, ten kilometres distant. But I have, as you see, a daughter. She has, you must have observed, talents of administration."

I had observed it. M. Nikels seemed himself to have little part in the management.

"My son, at the age of fourteen, was a great gourmet, and at table we used to tell him he really ought to be a chef. He took us seriously and ran away from home at the age of sixteen to study with the great chefs of Paris. He remained two years; there was no dissuading him. . . . He insisted on becoming a professional cook. Horticulture interests him, alas, not at all. His career in Paris would have been slow. Now, it chanced that the owner of this house (he really owns the castle, too, on the hill, but it is too expensive to heat in the winter) lost a great deal of money at Monte Carlo. He offered to rent us this villa. It seemed to us it would make an admirable hotel. It would give me and my daughter something to do (I am not allowed to garden any more) and we would have an expert chef at our disposal, and my son, too, would have a profession. My heart is not what it used to be, so I merely oversee things; my daughter is the director; my son is the chef. It is a well-run hotel, do you not think?"

I agreed heartily.

"As I am not allowed to do much these days in the horticultural line, I leave that to my wife. I still cultivate roses here." The garden was filled with the tallest and largest roses, the most intensely red roses I had ever seen.

"It is a pleasant life," said M. Nikels. He admitted that it was a little confining. In his youth, he had been gardener on great estates in Poland and Russia. His family did not understand his love of travel. They were content with Luxembourg, and so, on the whole, was he. But memories of journeys abroad sometimes assailed him and then he must travel, if only to Liége. Did I know Liége? No, I did not. Well, there were some points of interest and a little international and exotic flavour; there were many returned colonials there.

We must go there together some time. Perhaps I had errands to do there. And he could show me the principal sights. I must have another vermouth with him. He always drank one early in the morning. After the smoke in the café the night before, "*ça clarifie la gorge.*"

One morning about a week later I was working according to a programme I had established for myself, in my room overlooking the rose garden. There was a knock on the door. M. Nikels appeared, brisk, and apparently intent upon urgent business.

"Tomorrow we must go to Liége," he announced. "I have need of a tropical costume. It has turned very warm. They have costumes fit for the tropics at Liége, for the returned colonials. You will accompany me?"

I was in one of those spells of work when it seems tempting Fate or one's dæmon to interrupt it. Liége, even under M. Nikels's guidance, seemed hardly sufficient temptation. I tried to explain that I was adhering strictly to a programme. M. Nikels seemed disappointed, almost aggrieved.

"You will never have a better opportunity to be conducted through Liége," he said. "I don't know when I shall be able to go another time. There is going to be more to be done in the hotel as the season progresses. And," he added, "I don't know when I can persuade my daughter again. She is quite strict about my going. She does not realize that travel broadens the mind."

After lunch, stirring my kirsch in my coffee, I found myself alone with Mlle. Nikels.

"Is it," she said, looking at me intently, "that my father interrupted your work this morning?"

"Yes, but it did not in the least matter," I said.

"You permit that I demand," she said, "what he wished of you?"

"He asked me to accompany him to Liége tomorrow."

"Ah," she said, raising her hands in irritation and horror, "he has again the *folie de voyage*. It assails him every six months or so. Sometimes it is Paris, sometimes it is Strasbourg; sometimes Liége. He was in his youth a great traveller. He grows very restless. He sometimes departs suddenly and we do not hear from him for a week. He is in Paris, or Nancy, or Strasbourg, usually in Liége. He says it hurts the spirit to live always in Luxembourg. He really should not travel alone; he is not very well." (I began to feel guilty about not accompanying him to Liége.)

Mlle. Nikels resumed her knitting and asked suddenly: "Monsieur, you have of an evening here observed M. Felens?"

I had indeed.

"He is a good type, you agree, do you not?"

I did agree. A somewhat heavy, honest-looking man, said to be an excellent dentist. He knew his *métier*, I said I understood, and was a fine gentleman, quite unlike, I felt like adding, the young lawyer, another of the skat-players, who, after studying law at the University of Louvain and two years' practice in the village of Clairvaux, had explained to me the other evening all the defects, moral and spiritual, of America.

"Yes, a good type," she said ruminatively, "but he lacks courage."

I did not quite see how the practice of dentistry in Clairvaux called for great displays of courage. I looked at her inquiringly.

"Yes," she continued, "he lacks courage. Courage is a great virtue in a man, do you not agree, monsieur?"

"Next to wisdom," I said, recalling Plato suddenly.

"M. Felens is a good man and one of taste," she continued, "and you observe, too, that he comes here regularly?"

"Every evening," I said.

"It is not solely for the purpose of playing skat," she said, looking at me appraisingly to see how much divination I had.

"I gathered that," I said.

"He comes principally to see me," she said. I usually went to bed before the skat game ended. I wondered how much of Mlle. Nikels he saw.

"Frankly," she said, "one sometimes talks to a stranger more than one talks to one's intimates. You are not involved in the affairs of Luxembourg. You are a philosopher. I feel that I can talk to you. You are discreet. You have human understanding. You have travelled, you must know the world; you have read the philosophers, you will comprehend."

"I am glad to be of service, mademoiselle, though one can travel and read the philosophers without understanding the world."

"For four years M. Felens has been thinking of marrying me, but he cannot bring himself to say so," she said. "He lacks courage."

"But why courage?" I said. "He must know that you are interested in him; even I could see that. You have eyes for no one else when he is here."

"Oh, he is not afraid of me. But do you know M. Kratzenberger?"

"Oh, yes," I replied, "the gentleman who conducts the general emporium in the village. I do not find him sympathetic." I could not help wondering why M. Felens was afraid of M. Kratzenberger, and what that had to do with his projected marriage.

"But you should know Mme. Kratzenberger," continued Mlle. Nikels. "She is indescribable, a deplorable woman; not beautiful but very tenacious. She would never forgive M. Felens. You see, frankly, monsieur, M. Felens has had—it is long ended—an affair with Mme. Kratzenberger; it is not secret—the whole village knows it. M. Kratzenberger himself knows it. M. Felens, *voyez*, is a *célibataire;* he has been many years so; he lives alone with an elderly housekeeper. Nature will have its way; to each man *sa quantité.* The affair is long ended, but Mme. Kratzenberger still holds a power over M. Felens. It lacks to him courage. One would think she would tear his eyes out. Each year he is almost on the point of asking me to marry him, and then a kind of hysteria seizes him; he is in a state of collapse. He must go off for a vacation. The other night after the skat game was over, he began on the general subject of marriage. He said it was really time for him to marry, and—the next evening he told me that he is even now contemplating a holiday in the Vosges, alone."

"Is there nothing you can do?" I suggested sympathetically. "You are a woman of firmness and resource."

"I am troubled," she said. "I do not wish to force him. I have been content to wait. But there are now two young advocates in Diekirch, both interested, both with careers before them. My mother points out to me, correctly, that I cannot wait for ever. One must found a home. That understands itself prettily."

I learned a day or two later that M. Felens had left for the Vosges. He did not return before I left the inn. I returned to the inn once a year later. Mlle. Nikels was still at the bar, still busy, and when not busy, knitting. . . . How was M. Felens? I asked. He was away, she said sadly, *en vacances,* in the Vosges—alone.

"Philosophy teaches resignation, does it not?" she asked.

"Some philosophies do," I said.

"I, too, have become a philosopher," she said sadly.

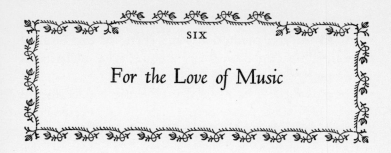

SIX

For the Love of Music

A PSYCHOLOGICAL inquiry ought to be made into the curious passion displayed by so many intellectual workers for the art of music. Any number of my friends turn from metaphysics to Mozart, and at the end of a day of academic routine or an evening's reading or writing find in ordered sound an escape from or a fulfilment of what they had sought, not successfully, in ideas.

It was midnight. I had been working all evening and found myself suddenly with that hunger for music which often at inconvenient hours assails the long-habituated lover of it. Heaven knows, one has enough music in New York. And now with that aristocrat among radio stations, WQXR, broadcasting the choicest records five hours a day, one need not even go to Carnegie or Town Hall. And I have, besides, a collection of records begun in the days when the phonograph companies regarded themselves as pioneers in recording on two sides of a record the second movement of Beethoven's *Fifth Symphony,* and continued until now when with time and money enough one can purchase the history of music on wax for festivals in one's own home. I could have put on a record; but I was lazy and tuned in on the radio instead, hoping against hope that at this unlikely hour there would be something worth listening to. WQXR was silent; the major stations were sending various swing bands into the midnight air. Suddenly, I could scarcely believe my ears: there was the sound of a symphony orchestra. I hesitated to turn on the volume very loud; after all it was midnight and the neighbours had once, at an earlier hour, complained when I had played quite loud (in a desperate desire to get the last barbarous violence over the loudspeaker) Stravinsky's *Sacre du Printemps*. I listened scrupulously. The low volume made careful listening necessary. The orchestral harmonies had a remote clarity, like music remembered in solitude or heard in a dream. But the dream was precise and steady now, and the details of orchestration clearer than I ever managed to hear them in memory, my musical recollection centring in themes that it is possible to hum or whistle. What could this be? Eighteenth century surely, Mozart or Haydn. One could not always be sure. There was one crude test. If it were Haydn one could be fairly certain at most given points what was going in essence to happen next. But that unexpected turn, that felicity, surprising but inevitable, like Aristotle's requisite for tragedy, that was Mozart, surely. But wait now. A long rising line, a deep musical exaltation, a sudden sharp descent, an inelegant, almost barbarous breadth and intensity; a phrase here that neither Haydn nor Mozart would have thought of, a modulation that suggested a range of consciousness and feeling in tone that could have been only one thing. "You have been listening," said the announcer, "to Beethoven's *Second Symphony*. It is part of a musical jamboree presented each night at this time by the Music Shop." I went to bed not unpleased with myself for having identified a style, and not sufficiently displeased for having failed to remember a symphony I had so long known.

And as often happens, not the themes of the symphony I had just heard, but by that strange process of associative musical excitement that listening seems to promote, the themes of everything else under the sun went through my head, and with them the times and the occasions I had heard them, and the whole world of music in which, as in a separate sphere, the music-lover lives. I have long envied those happy children who hear their mother play Bach fugues while they play with their toy trains in the living-room. I heard my sister play Beethoven, four hands, with a friend, but that was after I had begun to hear music for myself, and the music was neither Beethoven nor Bach. In Asbury Park, New Jersey, in the years from 1905 to 1911, on the Arcade on the boardwalk, there was provision for the musical hungers of the summer visitors. Plenty of provision, too, for there were fourteen concerts a week, each day at three o'clock and eight-fifteen. Except on state occasions I went to the afternoon concerts. I always had the impression that the evening programmes were choicer, and I hope they were. I cannot remember any one programme in its completeness. But I remember the star things, the *Poet and Peasant* Overture, the *Tannhäuser* Overture, Victor Herbert fantasias, Fantasia from *Rigoletto*, Rossini's *Wilhelm Tell* Overture, Nevin's "The Rosary" as a cornet solo (always repeated, sometimes twice, for the benefit of the small but enthusiastic audience that turned up on weekday August afternoons). Arthur Pryor, immaculate and tall in his white bandmaster's costume, seemed to me what Toscanini came to seem to me later, and though I vaguely felt it might have been nice if this band had had strings, I didn't miss them much. What time I could spare from seeing how far along the Jersey coast I could get by bicycle or inter-urban trolley, I spent learning about music from Arthur Pryor and his band. I wish that debonair leader were still alive. I should like to write to thank him for initiating me into concerted music. I have since heard more sophisticated bands that have dug up great seventeenth-century chorales for brass instruments, but the *Poet and Peasant* Overture played on a sultry August Thursday on the old Arcade Pier at Asbury Park was my first intimation of what could be done by sounding brass and tinkling cymbals. I have heard Heifetz play the Brahms Concerto with the Philharmonic under Toscanini, but, make no mistake about it, the cornetist of Pryor's band could wring our hearts at the old Arcade with a cornet version of "Angel's Serenade." At any rate, he wrung mine, and once it deliriously seemed to me that the third time he repeated it, he was doing it for the benefit of one small boy rapturously applauding in the first row. As least he smiled, and I thought at me.

It is a familiar psychological conception, made current by William James, that every sensation tends to go over into a motor response. After listening to Arthur Pryor and his band a whole summer, I felt I must do something with music myself. My sister was already studying the piano, so it seemed sensible that I should study the violin. It was the days before good phonographs and records, and one knew families that had whole concerts at home because children in the family could play two instruments. My playing was not a great success. I like to blame my bad eyes, which made it quite diffi-

cult for me to see the notes and hold the violin in proper
position at the same time. I certainly do not blame Edgar
Allan Deutsch, the excellent teacher, an old friend of my
aunt, who was entrusted with the thankless task of teaching
me how to hold the bow, how to finger, to read musical
notation, to put rosin on my bow, and to distinguish the first
from the fourth position. I don't think I ever advanced as far
as the fourth position. But Edgar Allan Deutsch was patient
and my family long-suffering. Mischa Elman, my mother
assured me, must have sounded bad at first. I ran into Mr.
Deutsch once at a Menuhin recital last year. We discussed
the "lost" Schumann Concerto which Menuhin had just
played. We agreed that Schumann was really great as a composer for the piano, even in his orchestral writing. We did
not think the lost Concerto was truly violinistic. We thought
it might well have been left lost. We had quite a discussion
on the requirements of good violin-playing. Mr. Deutsch
was very kind about not mentioning my wretchedly brief
career as a violinist and talked to me almost as to a fellow-
musician. It was very generous of him. For I nearly ruined a
concert of his once.

The spring of the season in which I studied with him he
had a concert given by his pupils. He took a chance on me.
I came to a rehearsal of the minuet of one of the Haydn symphonies. I have ever since had a sense of the feeling that a
member of an orchestra must have when things go well, a
wonderful, mystical thrill of unanimity in creation. I was
lifted by the sense of concerted momentum, all those strings
playing divinely together. I admit I thought my violin
sounded a little different from the rest, and I seemed to be
a few notes behind everybody else. I started to hurry. Mr.

Deutsch stopped us. He whispered to me that perhaps I'd better sit down on a bench at the side and watch the others, and listen. That is what I have been doing at concerts ever since. Except for a pianola in a summer camp, I have never done anything remotely like musical performance since. But none of the great conductors can have had a grander sense of command than I did at the shabby pianola in a wooden playhouse in the Adirondacks, playing away at the *Fifth Symphony,* modifying tempo to suit myself, pumping energy with my feet into my imaginary orchestra and deciding then, as I have often decided since, that being a conductor of a great orchestra is the *ne plus ultra* in glory and power.

My serious listening career began in the days when Josef Stransky was conducting the New York Philharmonic Orchestra. I think I knew even then that I was not listening to a great conductor, nor did all of it at the time seem to me great music. There seems to have been a clause in a bequest by Joseph Pulitzer to the Philharmonic which specified that a certain amount of Liszt and Tchaikovsky must be played. I don't know how many times through high school and college I heard Liszt's *Les Préludes.* I once almost learnt by heart the poem by Lamartine which constituted, or was said to constitute, its libretto. They don't play Liszt's *Les Préludes* much any more, and I doubt if it would seem to many young men today to be the meditation in music, the philosophy, romantic, sighing, and grandiloquent, that at the age of sixteen it seemed to me to be. The young music-lovers I know have found nobler food for austere emotions in Bach's *Passacaglia in C Minor,* in the *St. Matthew Passion,* in the Brahms *Requiem.* But there used to be sixty-year-olds in the audience who seemed to feel about Liszt as I did. And the dying falls of the violins, the pleading woodwinds that moaned wistfully through the second movement of Tchaikovsky's *Fifth Symphony,* gave me—gave a whole generation of young lovers of music—emotions which, if not the most purely musical, were as pure in their directness and sincerity and absorption as those evoked in a brighter, more musically experienced youth by national broadcasts of Bach and Purcell, Gluck and Mozart. Perhaps more so.

One cannot help envying the young now growing up with the opportunity of hearing music everywhere and at almost any time. How eagerly one used to wait, twenty-five years ago, for a chance to hear again a symphony just discovered, a musical love for the first time experienced and aroused. The César Franck symphony—could it have seemed such a revelation once?—played on a Sunday afternoon in Carnegie Hall. The familiar third theme of the first movement came as an announcement of a spirit speaking, clear and bold, and as it rose in full orchestra in the last part of the first movement and reappeared, triumphantly surging above a counter-theme in the third, one young listener felt a new world of sound and of thought had been opened to him. When might one hear it again! There were no records; there was no radio. And it might be months before it would be played again. The César Franck *D Minor Symphony* seems banal now, and that majestic theme appearing finally in full and lucid brass sounds less majestic than it used to do, and it reappears too often throughout. One can hear it, or better music, over and over again, lounging at home on a Sunday afternoon, or over a dozen different radio stations during the week. It is a great boon, doubtless, to be able to hear the symphonies time and again, interrupted by the telephone, by visitors, by a sense that one doesn't have to listen at all, by the consciousness that this is not a major event. Music has ceased to be something sacramental and eventful and has become the familiar staple, the *carte du jour,* of our lives. The young music-lover of today knows all the themes far better than his predecessor of twenty years ago. He hears Beethoven at four, at five, at midnight, on cigarette and bank programmes; he does not need the announcer to tell him it is a Bach concerto or a Schumann sonata. But he also does not have the sense of a high and signal occasion that music meant to us in the days before the phonograph and the radio put it as casually as a news bulletin in our homes. *Eheu fugues, eheu fugues,* one almost is tempted to say, summoning up the musical memories that were musical events.

What made the event was not always the fame or the mastery of the conductor or the virtuosity of the strings. I have read æstheticians who write learnedly and emphatically about immediate experiences as the great thing in the experience of art. But they forget to tell us that what helps to constitute the immediate experience of a work of art is the mood in which it is approached and the context in which it is apprehended. It is not, I am sure, the performance of *Pelléas and Mélisande* that was so distinguished one June night many years ago at the Opéra Comique. No orchestra can be delicate enough to do justice to the nuanced hypnosis of that subtly breathing score. Pelléas was not the diffident, half faunlike, half angelic lover he should have been, nor Mélisande exactly a *"princesse lointaine"* of remote pathos and tragic shadows. But before the tenuous, firm delicacies of the prelude there had been another prelude, a dinner in a good restaurant with a golden wine and in the company of an old friend in good spirits, on a summer evening in Paris. We were both a little *exaltés*, and neither of us, I think, had ever heard *Pelléas* on the stage before. I think we would have been prepared to find anything beautiful, but that *Pelléas* on a summer evening seemed, as it has done since, sheer enchantment. It was bathed in a shimmering twilight of exact and preternaturally poignant perception. The wonder was in Debussy, but it was also in the wine and in ourselves. Even at the Metropolitan—dissipated in the cavernous spaces of the Metropolitan—*Pelléas* is a hypnosis as much as it is music. But *Pelléas* is always to me a summer evening in Paris; and when Golaud sings about the tragic heart of man, it is always summer and the Opéra Comique and a golden wine and a good friend. Or again, I have heard, even over the radio, much better performances of Brahms's *Third Symphony* than I heard over the radio of a hotel bar on a bitter cold January afternoon in Palermo. A solitary Italian was throwing dice to amuse himself. It was all I could do to hear. But I had been five weeks without music, and suddenly, after the announcement of some racing returns had been given, a voice calmly announced the *Terza Sinfonia* of Brahms. It was manna from heaven. *The Power of Sound* is the name of a book published some sixty years ago, one of the now dated analyses of the æsthetics of music. I do not know when I felt its power more. One may say what one will about the inadequacy of the radio: that it is stereoscopic; that there is not the edge and tang of an actual performance heard in the concert hall; that the choirs do not come properly balanced (Olin Downes once explained all that in a review of a Toscanini radio concert). This remains: the music in a kind of distilled essence is there; listening to it alone, for its own sake,

one discovers its articulate form and becomes sometimes,
more than in a concert hall, one with it. Henry Adams remarks somewhere that all he got out of his stay in Germany
was Beethoven by accident in a German beer garden. Of
Palermo, next to Monreale, I remember chiefly the *Third
Symphony* of Brahms, the benedictive reappearance in its
closing passage of the theme first uttered with vigour by the
whole orchestra in the opening of the first movement. And
suddenly I remember, too, the evening in Carnegie Hall when
that touch of genius in the composition was first pointed out
to me by a friend. And the night, too, when, too tired to
listen, I heard Toscanini conduct the same symphony and
heard only the sounds, and I am certain not all of those.

And I must add two more instances of circumstantial listening. Adolf Busch is a great though unrhetorical artist and the
Bach *Violin Concerto* is great music. But would I remember
it as well, I wonder, save for the accident that gave me, like
the mad King Ludwig, a whole theatre to myself to hear it
in? Luck had first given me the opportunity to hear Busch
and his quartet at a private home in Oxford, and luck too
brought me together with him in Rome. I had just finished
hearing Busch and Serkin play a sonata recital at Santa
Cecilia and had decided that chamber music was the purest
form of music: in it a composer had to say what he has to
say without any extravagance of instrumentation. He cannot
conceal poverty by sheer physical power of massed instruments. I had been deeply moved by two players, one a poet
and one a scholar, who played nothing but Bach, Beethoven,
and Mendelssohn. Busch, Serkin, and I had dinner together
and Serkin left for a concert in Vienna. "Would you like,"
Adolf Busch asked, "to come to a rehearsal with me? I am

playing a series of three concerti with the Augusteo Orchestra on Sunday, and we are having a dress rehearsal tonight."

"Three concerti! Good God!" I exclaimed.

It *was* a dress rehearsal. Except for two or three pauses, accompanied by a mutter of conversation between the young conductor and Adolf Busch, the three concerti were played straight through. Except that there was no audience but my fortunate self in the old amphitheatre that had been made into a concert hall, it might have been the concert itself. All the pleasures of solitude were there, combined with all the urgency and volume of an actual performance. There are all sorts of prerogatives of enormous wealth—sailing the ocean in lonely splendour on a yacht, or having a vast wooded estate to wander over with a few chosen friends. I am now inclined to think I should waive all that for the pleasure of indulging in a concert orchestra and having a virtuoso play Bach, Beethoven, and Mendelssohn (I should perhaps waive the Mendelssohn) for me and perhaps for a few humanists like, say, M. Platon.

One final instance. I have a friend, Andrew Tietjen, the assistant organist at St. Thomas's in New York, who asked me one evening whether I should like to hear some Bach on the great organ in the church.

"Lie down on one of the pews, if you like," he said when I arrived at the church. "There's nobody here."

So for more than an hour in the shadows of the half-lighted nave, I lay listening to unobtrusive chorales, preludes, and fugues. Andrew plays well, purely and with style. The waves of sound came pouring and swelling into the auditorium, and before long there was no organist; there was no listener; there was only music being played, music being listened to, and the music and the listening were one. Those measured chords of disciplined passion were pure spirit—Bach's spirit translated into sound. I am not sure that it was after that evening that I wrote these lines. But it must have been an evening very like it:

> *The feeling hidden here in robes of state*
> *Goes marching strictly to a formal beat*
> *Without parade of passion, without heat*
> *Of agony untamed and inchoate.*
> *Here is no puerile bleating against fate,*
> *No love that sobs melodious in defeat;*
> *These measures do not stridently repeat*
> *In sound the substance of an ancient hate.*
> *Here a spirit speaking pure and clear,*
> *But cool, and with such courteous control*
> *The ear itself must first be schooled to hear*
> *This music's fragments and discern the whole,*
> *The rapture rising definite and sheer*
> *From depths of the serene and private soul.*

But, of course, one generally hears music with other people; even when one is alone at a concert there is an incalculable osmosis of feeling from the audience. On some occasions, as part of an audience hearing great music greatly played, I have had the sense (and I suspect that I am not alone) of participating in a rite rather than attending a concert, a feeling of having a communion not only with the music—a moment's absorption in timeless and discarnate beauty—but a rapt identification with others sharing that communion. It is an illusion doubtless, as the lady in the row behind me, making comments in the pauses on the conductor's latest divorce, would be the first to agree. But one cannot help, none the less, remembering the suggestions made by many philosophers, beginning with Plato, that the exposure to beautiful sights and sounds must inevitably raise the spirit and refine the temper of those who hear and see them, and make them communicants, at once vivid and disinterested, of the same divine order. One likes to fancy with Plato (who, as Socrates, says that philosophy is simply a finer kind of music) that the wide spread of the love of the art of music is a hopeful symptom, an aspiration toward harmony in an unharmonious world. Minds at one in the clear tonal patterns of Mozart must come to relish peace and pattern in their lives. Millions of listeners listening to Toscanini conduct the *Ninth Symphony* must all become brothers in joy. It is an attractive thesis and I should be ready to welcome it if I did not remember the amount of snobbish cant, of stupidity and malice, one can hear the moment Koussevitzky drops his baton at Carnegie Hall or Toscanini his in the Salzburg that was. But perhaps that splendid lady in her jewels was not listening to the music at all, perhaps that Maharajah came from India to Salzburg to be seen rather than to hear. Thursday evening in Carnegie you can find gathered the elect and powerful of the city of New York, and at Salzburg in its great pre-Nazi days the elect of the world. But the world goes on much as it was, full of stratagems and spoils. Perhaps the music does insinuate itself into the souls of the elect. Or perhaps, if only for a moment, the stratagems and spoils are stilled. The Berlin Philharmonic is said still to be very fine, and there are audiences to listen to it. Plato imagined that the beauty of music might be an anagram of the beauty of the universe, the music of the spheres overhead. But perhaps he was wrong. Perhaps, as St. Paul said of the wisdom he taught: it is not of this world. Can that be the reason audiences, composed so often of the worldly and the disillusioned, love it so much? If they do.

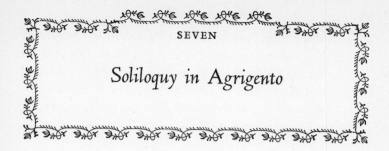

SEVEN

Soliloquy in Agrigento

E VER since, in 1921, good luck had enabled me to make
the grand tour and the grand tour had included Agrigento, I had wanted to come back to it. That sunlit afternoon
in January before the temple of Juno facing the sea had been
for me an image of Greece, more than anything, almost, in
Greece itself. I must come back here some day, I had said to
myself, and, with the rhetorical tragedy youth indulges in,
I had murmured that I never should. These ruined, beautiful,
sandstone columns were the echo of a vanished civilization,
in this island whose landscapes and light were also a memorial to Greece. The chances of coming back seemed literally
remote in time; a young instructor does not think as far as
sabbaticals. Moreover, the air was full in those post-war
years, as it is today, of the end of European civilization itself.
Who knows; it might never be possible to come back here
again. The image must be fixed for ever. I tried to fix it in
a sonnet which I give here, not as literature but as the recollection of a moment in time, a memory in the life of a young
American by Sicily rendered homesick—for Greece.

And after all what is there here to thrill
The senses, what live beauty here that sings
Deep to the heart? Ruined temples on a hill,
Passion and pathos of dead perfect things,
Golden brown columns, rhythmic spaces, blue
That throbs intensely in the sky and sea;
Soft rolling mountains and the reddening hue
Of sun on sandstone. What else can there be?
Or do there loiter in this falling light,
White slender forms that once made music here?
Do we catch echoes on the wind tonight
Of unstilled voices rising cool and clear?
  Or do the young gods once more as we gaze
  Stand bright and breathing in the twilight haze?

Here, seventeen years later, I was back again, only to feel
the changes that time had made; nor were those changes
wholly in myself. The changes were certainly not in the
temples; Concordia rose as magnificent and massive as ever,
the sandstone of its columns framing the still incredible blue.
There was a silver of almond blossoms all over the landscape,
but there would have been those seventeen years ago, too,
if I had come in March instead of in January. The Hôtel des
Temples was not changed. But it seemed less remote than
it used to do before the charabancs and the *torpedine* train
had made Girgenti, now Agrigento, only a stone's throw
from Palermo; the sarcophagus in the cathedral was as lovely,
as superb a fifth-century bas-relief as ever; the light as clean,
exact, and clear; and the hills the same dark, almost desolate
green, accenting the blue of the sea.

The town had changed, and perhaps I noticed it more. The

year I had been here last was the year before the Anno Primo
of the Fascist regime. There had been then no fine motor
road to Palermo; the insolently handsome modernistic post-
office, the streamlined cafés, had not been present. The streets
had been dirtier. But there had also been a blessed absence
of monumental carvings on all the walls, reminding one *ad
nauseam* of the existence of the Duce and including such
heroical sentiments as *Live dangerously; One must be willing
to die for one's faith; Fascism is not a party but a religion.* There
were still the donkey-carts, but their owners at that time had
not worn Fascist buttons. The peasants still sang, but then
there had been no black shirts, and "Giovinezza" with its
horrible banality could not have been heard on the island.

Those temples are more than ever an image and concentration of Greece: open to the sun and facing the sea and this
clear and candid sky; innocent, as Greek religion had not
been before the Olympian period, of the mystery of the
suffering god; and untouched by the distrust of natural life
and the fears of after-death that were to sweep the world
with Christianity. The goats, whose descendants still wander
around the temples and among the tourists from the barbarous and unknown North, were slaughtered as sacrifices; but
the desires and impulses of men, and their enjoyments, were
not maimed or killed so that they might be one with the discarnate pure Being, in union with whom was their beatitude.

I was a little less tempted, even in the intense noon sunlight that bathed these columns in an aureole of singing
peace, to believe, as I had once believed, that Greek life had
burned always with a hard, gemlike flame, lived by perfect-
proportioned, clean-limbed, heroic men and women, all
white loveliness in draperies as flowing and ethereal as those

on the sarcophagus in the cathedral in town. The cathedral itself was a church built on a Greek temple, as Christianity had been superimposed on Greek thought and feeling, and had hidden but not replaced or destroyed it. I knew a little more now about what a sly, adventurous, imperialistic, fighting, quarrelsome set of little rival polities those Greek cities had been, and a good deal more about the seamy side of the Greek way, the slavery that underlay its aristocracy, the perversity that poisoned its love. I had sighed the January evening I had been here seventeen years before, standing among the columns (but a few remain) of the temple of Juno. The end of the day had seemed to me the end of a world, and the world that was ending for me had been one that had ended two thousand years ago. But what had I sighed for and what had ended? I now asked myself. The best of Greek life, or something at least of the best of it, has survived. There died with Greece as much cruelty and barbarism and stupidity as continue to live in our own. More sadness lay for me now in the thought: when our world, too, should have vanished, what fragment would an archæ-ologist or a tourist find two thousand years later that would make him homesick for our civilization, as all who come here are made homesick for Greece?

The ruins of the temple of Juno were not the only frag-ments that came to mind here at Agrigento. Had not Em-pedocles lived here once, though, according to legend, it was at Etna that he ended his life? The elderly tourists, after a glimpse at the Greek temples, go to Taormina, too, in Etna's shadow. Here by this blue sea, on this fertile earth, in this beautiful life-giving sun, and breathing this crystal air, Em-pedocles might well have guessed that all is earth, air, fire, and water; and among a people whose passions must have been as intense as the eyes of these Sicilian peasants, it is not surprising that he should have hit upon love and hate as the twin principles that brought things to birth and death respectively. Philosophy has now long been the preoccupation of teachers in academies, arguing about the words they expressly invent and the problems they professionally create. Their systems, like Hegel's, for instance, remain in perfect wholes; of the early Greeks we have only fragments, but fragments of spirits that framed their cosmic divinations as to the nature of things on olive-clad hilltops, in the sunlight, by temples built to genial gods; finite men dreaming in these wide spaces of infinite distances and of ultimate things, and of divine beings, not to be taken too seriously, save as poetic images of perfection.

But the Greek thinkers were not prophetic souls dreaming on things to come. Surely they could not have dreamt of these Germans now approaching the temple, their guide-books in hand, counting the columns to be sure there were the right number, and commenting, not exactly with unction, that they were "*kolossal!*" They could not have dreamt of the elderly Americans here yesterday from Boston who seemed so tired and careworn from travels they did not have to take and who complained sadly that, though they were interested in art and all that sort of thing, they were weary of seeing so many old things: the Greek theatre at Taormina, the Greek temple at Segesta, the quarries at Syracuse, and there was a Greek theatre there, too! Nor was it likely that they foresaw the young Swede who picked up a piece of pottery, obviously factory-made and also obviously not more than two years old, hoping against hope to smuggle it out of the country despite the law against the exportation of antiquities.

There was so much more, too, that the Greek philosopher could not have foreseen, or he might have said that, given our post-war power politics, it was the principle of hate by which the world was moved.

Legend has it that Empedocles, too, was a kind of dictator; perhaps he might not have been surprised after all by the regime, half violence and half rhetoric, which now included and obsessed this beautiful island. Plato surely would have understood a commonwealth which said that the individual found his fulfilment only in the State, but he would not have understood this State in which it was brute, megalomaniac power rather than disinterested wisdom that ruled.

And would Empedocles have made more than do some of the contemporary Sicilians of these wanderers from the North who come here to bask in the sun and in the past? The priest who shows you the tombstone in the cathedral asks about the skyscrapers in New York. The schoolboys whom I talked with yesterday wondered why all these Englishmen and Germans and Americans came here to look at a few foolish columns. Meanwhile, the people in the hotel talk with alarm of China, of Austria, of Spain; some Americans yesterday talked about hurrying home. One walks down to the temples at sunset; there is no one there. There is simply a façade of symmetry, an image of order, built by perishing men two thousand years ago against a changing but eternal sea, a moment of time made into a monument of eternity; and men and women come here from a troubled world to a picture—it is only a picture—of security and peace.

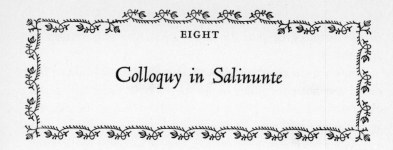

EIGHT

Colloquy in Salinunte

A PROFESSOR goes abroad and leaves behind him his library and his lecture notes, his colleagues and his students. But he is for ever reminded of them, especially of the last, for time and again in Europe one recognizes the young collegian as various as he is on the campus. If he is the collegiate Babbitt, he continues fraternity life on shipboard, or exuberantly destroys or enlivens the demure quiet of an English village inn. One sees him sometimes in the galleries or churches, continuing on the ground itself his course in the History of Art.

Carl had turned up in Agrigento, intending to stay only a day. He had stayed twelve. It was part of the Grand Tour which had begun, as he put it, with romance—not too serious—in Paris, and had carried him as far as Timbuktu. He had only just completed his course at one of the better and more fashionable New England colleges—more precisely, Amherst. He was a nice boy—you could see that at a glance in his candid blue eyes and his clear features; and an intelligent and sensitive one—you could tell that after ten minutes' conversation with him. In his last year at college he had become fascinated with the history of art; outside of his fraternity, one or two teachers, and one or two friends, college had not aroused his intelligence or his feelings very much. But art history had aroused both. He had gone so far as to get himself admitted to graduate work in Fine Arts at Harvard, but his father, a prominent lawyer in a Middle-Western city, had dissuaded him. Then he must have a year abroad, he had said to his father. "What would be the tangible results of that?" his father had asked him, patiently; Carl was an only child. Carl had not been able to explain. It might give him enough art for a lifetime, he had told his father; "I wouldn't mind so much going into law." And here he was in Agrigento. He had intended simply to have a look at it and then rush on, like everyone else, to Syracuse. But something about the clear beauty of the temple, its definiteness, the luxury of the fertile landscape after the impressive but bleak desert spaces he had been through for weeks in North Africa, had prompted him to stay. The temples had a fascination for him. He must see them at midday and at twilight and in the evening. They not only moved him, but excited his curiosity. He knew a good deal about Greek orders but little about Greek religion. He said he must find out more when he returned home.

"How about going to Salinunte?" I said. "There's said to be a magnificent temple there, more grand and extensive than the one here. We might go together. One needs to hire a car, but a car would not be very expensive if we shared the expense."

Carl was delighted, and by noon the next day we were eating our lunch in a cool corner of the temple, among the

Sicilian goats and lizards, observed, at as close range as they felt they dared, by two curious dark Sicilian boys.

"There's a lot I didn't get at college," Carl said as he leaned against a column sleepily, after drinking a whole bottle of red wine.

"What, for instance?"

"Well, Greek philosophy and Greek religion; a lot that you were telling me about yesterday."

"You could have gotten it," I said; "there's a perfectly good course in that at Amherst."

"Oh, I know; and it's a good college, mind you. I'm homesick for it already. But people think you are kind of queer if you take things too seriously, and philosophy's rather highbrow at college. If you go in for that kind of thing, they think you're rather sad."

"Rather *what?*" I said.

"Oh, *sad* is a technical term; it's the opposite of tops."

"Oh, I see; and if you're interested in ideas you're *sad.*"

"That's right. But, mind you, I got a good deal. You thought me ignorant yesterday because I didn't know who Heraclitus was. But there are some things I do know. Try me on the Treaty of Utrecht and the Diet of Worms and Savonarola. I was just trying to think of things you might not know as much about as you seem to about Greek ideas. And then there was the fraternity, and the dances, and the bull sessions. It was a really wonderful four years. And you confess I did learn something about the history of art. But I wish I could have my last two years over again. I'd know what to do with them now."

"Do you want to be a lawyer?" I asked.

"I think I do; and it would please my father. But most of

all I'd like to keep alive, as alive as I feel here, and have as
much to keep me alive. Does all this fade as one grows
older?" He waved rather comprehensively at the sea, at the
tremendous columns that almost suggested Egypt and Rome,
Karnak and Baalbek, rather than Greece.

"A little," I said; "and there are no Greek temples in
Ohio."

"Oh, I don't mean Greek temples," he said. "I mean what
one feels in their presence. I imagine much of that goes. You
ought to know; you are almost twice my age. Am I likely
to become like that Boston insurance man and his wife here
yesterday, tired and bored?"

"Oh, it doesn't all go, especially if life doesn't press you
too hard—and I judge it's not likely to with you. You've
got a pretty smooth career laid out for you, and have had a
pretty smooth time all your life. Though, as you may have
heard, it's a changing world, and the economic system which
sent you to college—the system which makes the kind of
college and collegiate ideals you knew—may not last your
lifetime, or it may be very considerably changed."

"I hope it isn't," he said, throwing a roll to the dogs and
holding out some sandwiches to the Sicilian boys.

"Why?"

"Selfishness, I suppose. I rather like the way the world is
arranged for people in the income group of my parents."

"You don't altogether like it," I said; "you told me so
yourself. That's the world of the Boston insurance agent you
mentioned, tired and bored and rather hard, didn't you
think?"

"*Very.* I'd hate to meet that man in his office," Carl replied. "But on the other hand, you really wouldn't want the

dullness of a collective society, would you"—one of the
Sicilian boys began to whistle "Giovinezza"—"or a Fascist
one?" he added.

"And what makes you think a collective society would be
dull?"

"Well, it wouldn't produce good manners and pleasant
people; you said you liked Amherst students."

"Yes, they're very nice; they're a type, though. Didn't you
just say they rather resented ideas or an interest in them as a
little queer? Didn't you tell me that you met at college just
about the same kind of people that you met at prep school?
Wouldn't you like a little more variety in the world than,
with all due respect, you met at Amherst or in your fraternity? And a brighter life than American boys of the privileged classes grow up into?"

"But," Carl said, looking steadily at one of the massive
columns, "the great things in art, I seem to have heard, were
all the product of an aristocratic tradition. They had slaves
in Greece, but slaves didn't direct the building of temples."

"American plutocrats, or the American middle class, have
still to produce great art, Carl."

"True; and I must say there is a good deal of dullness in
the society I grew up in. And I admit I grow furious when
I hear the way the people in our town talk. I'm a regular
Red next to them."

"Even compared with the factory workers? There are a
lot of them in your city."

"Well, I confess I don't know many."

"And while we are on the subject of the middle class,
doesn't it seem rather a pity that the facilities of a good college should be largely devoted to young men whose parents

happen to be financially able to send them there? There might be a livelier intellectual atmosphere in American colleges if we were living in a society where all young men with the brains to justify an education got it, and nobody else. It seems to me I read the other day that the President of Harvard, not a rabid revolutionary, said just that."

"I might not have been admitted," Carl said, smiling, "if they enforced that very strictly. But to get back to my original question—the system *may* last my lifetime—am I likely to be as dull as that insurance broker from Boston? Will I be bored by these temples thirty years from now, or by music, or by ideas or people?"

"No," I said, looking at his eager and generous face. "I don't think you will be."

"I'd rather be killed in a war first. Well, there's a good chance I may be. Boy!" he said, jumping up suddenly and flinging out his arms and breathing deeply, as if he would inhale the temple and the sunlight and the sea. "I bet I'll remember this next March in the Yale Law School."

"You'll remember it longer than that," I said.

I thought suddenly of George Gissing, in the bitterness and squalor of poverty in a London winter, living in memory and imagination "by the Ionian sea," and of how many minds, engulfed or perplexed by the modern world, remembering Greece.

NINE

The Author Is Mistaken for An English Poet in Corinth

EVERYONE with a love of poetry or sculpture or of the past wishes to come to Greece, but I had found a special excuse for myself to go to one part of it.

"If you are following in the footsteps of St. Paul," I said to myself one morning in Athens, "you must go to Corinth." (I was writing a little book designed to display the mystic that lay at the heart of the missionary.) It is an easy trip: three hours; but nobody had told me that it is over ten miles to the ruins of the ancient Corinth I wanted to see. At the railway-station was a lonely car, apparently for hire. I tried immediately that French which I had found to be a *lingua franca* in modern Greece, at least in the places tourists are likely to go.

The chauffeur replied in French; we fixed a price; and just as I was about to get in, he looked at me narrowly and said in a kind of English I had last heard in the Candy Kitchens of Saratoga Springs and Amherst, Mass.:

"You are English. . . ."

It was not a question but a statement, with just a touch of

accusation and the implication that my speaking French was
an attempt, not very successful, to disguise the fact.

"No," I replied in English. "I am American."

"You are English," the driver insisted, "you are an English poet! It's no use denying it; I know."

Now there was enough of a compliment in both the noun
and in the adjective or, at least, in the two in combination,
to make me feel almost pleased. It was inspiriting to have a
casual taxi-driver recognize the spirit and temper that had
brought me to Greece. I had written verse, and when professional philosophical colleagues wished to pay me an ambiguous compliment, they had called me a poet. Poets, too, are
vague, and are allowed lapses in logic. And I myself had always regarded philosophy as a peculiarly serious and comprehensive kind of poetry. But I did not suppose this citizen
of Corinth had reflected on all these matters (after all, he
was not an ancient Greek; indeed, he was a very young one).
Moreover, though we were near many ancient shrines, I did
not think that the spirit of the mysteries had so entered into
him that he could by a momentary glance intuit the spirit of
poetry in my face. "You are a poet," somebody had said to
me once after reading what I had intended as a piece of exact
æsthetic analysis. But this chap repeated: "You are an English poet," with the dogmatic matter-of-factness of a police
officer saying: "You are an English pickpocket," and the insistence of a detective who suspected I was trying to conceal
my identity.

I had often been mistaken for an Englishman, especially in
Italy, where in certain small villages you can spend hours in
vain explaining that England and the United States are three
thousand miles apart, that the temperament of the two peo-

ples differs, that even the language is not the same, and be told at the end: "None the less, it's all equal—English, American, *tutti inglesi*." Then they all ask for Three Castles cigarettes, or Lucky Strikes.

"No," I repeated, "I am not an English poet. In the first place, I am an American; in the second place, I am a professor, not a poet." I thought I had him there.

"Are you sure you are not English?" he said, looking at me very searchingly. I was wearing grey flannels and a blue jacket that, with the proper college insignia, might have passed for an Oxford blazer. I was carrying the *Manchester Guardian*, too, which I had borrowed from an Englishman in the hotel at Athens. It looked a little suspicious, but my accent surely did not sound so.

"No," I said, "I am American."

"You are young," he said reflectively. Even there he was wrong. "A young English poet. Tell the truth, won't you?" There was a note, half-plea, half-threat, in his voice.

I dug into my pocket and, disentangling my passport from my letter of credit and my Traveller's Map of Greece, opened it to the not incredible photograph of myself upon it.

"There," I said, "that ought to settle it. There's my passport picture."

He examined it with care and then proceeded to hunt in the seat beside him for documents of his own. He finally produced one—a Greek newspaper with a fairly large photograph on its front page. It was the picture, not very clear, of a youngish-looking man who did look not *much* less like me than I liked to believe did my passport photograph.

"You are sure that isn't you?" the driver persisted. "It looks more like you than that passport photo does."

"No," I said, "it isn't. But who is it? I can't read modern Greek and why are you so interested in proving that I am the man in that picture? Is he an escaped criminal?"

"No, not a criminal," he said, "an English poet—young, rich, lost. I was sure I had found him." The chauffeur seemed very sad.

"An English poet—young, rich, lost," I repeated. "What do you mean—lost?"

"Lost himself," he said, "in the mountains, on Olympus, people say. Wished to get away from everybody, from his family, from himself, from the English. Lost himself weeks ago. . . . Family very worried. Offer large reward. Everybody in Greece looking for him. I was sure I had found him," he repeated, looking quite chagrined.

"I'm terribly sorry I can't oblige," I said. "But let's get on to Corinth." We did, and in the short drive and while pottering about the ruins where I tried to imagine Paul speaking on the Unknown God, I could not help thinking about the young English poet who had tried to lose himself on Olympus; tried to get away from everybody—from his family, from himself, from the English—and of the large reward offered by his parents to bring him back to his family, possibly, they thought, back to himself. A theme for meditation. I made a note of it, thinking I might use it some day, in a moral tale. In how many wealthy families have young men not tried to lose themselves on Olympus and been brought to earth by a reward or a constraint, or both? I could not help feeling a little pride in having been mistaken for a poet who had tried to escape the world of Philistinism, or bourgeois responsibility or routine. An English poet deliberately lost in Greece.

Not a bad description of Keats, of Shelley, of much of
A. E. Housman, of Matthew Arnold. Would ancient Greeks,
like the modern ones, I wondered, have tried to return this
poet to his family? Or would the gods have kept him on
Olympus? Were they keeping him now?

I had seen all that anyone but an archæologist could see
among the ruins. The driver approached with a suggestion:
if I were going back to Athens, would I ride back with him?
It was a beautiful drive along the coast, much better than by
train. He had to go to Athens anyway and would take me
for very few drachmas. It seemed a happy idea. It was, despite the holes in the road, a beautiful drive along the Aegean.
The clear outlines of the Greek coast and mountains are
made for the mind wishing for a time to be bathed in the
Hellenic world. I was consumed with the lights and shadows
and the memories of the sound that Sophocles heard long
ago on the Aegean, "bringing the eternal note of sadness
in." The shadows lengthened. The driver turned to me.
"Would you like to stop at Eleusis?" he said, as casually as a
taxi-driver in New York might ask if one wished to stop at
Grant's Tomb. "It's on our way." *Would* I!

In Greece one ought to be, or be with, an archæologist.
But the stones in the dying sunlight spoke of many things
that Plato and Euripides had spoken of, and I wandered,
happily lost, in my own way and for the moment a poet lost
in Greece. The uniformed guard had left me and had walked
outside the gates of the ruins to talk with the chauffeur.
When I finally came out, I found the two of them in what
seemed violent altercation.

"What's the trouble?" I said in English to the chauffeur.

"He says," he remarked heatedly, "that you are that young

English poet for whom a reward is offered. I told him he's foolish; you are an American professor. Very different."

"Very different indeed," I said.

We arrived at Athens by dark. The chauffeur had been regaling me with memories of Coney Island, a Greek lost in modernity, while I, only half paying attention, my eyes fixed on the fading landscape, tried to lose myself in Greece.

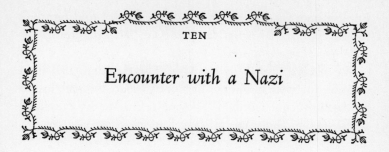

TEN

Encounter with a Nazi

A SABBATICAL leave is a professor's chance to get away
from it all. It was on the terrace of the Hôtel des
Temples at Agrigento, facing the Greek temples and the sea.
I might have thought the prospect the perfect image of
Hellenic serenity, had I not just that moment finished reading in the London *Times* the account of the rape of Austria.
The geniality of the scene did not consort with the brutal
political landscape of Europe, of which even here one could
not help being reminded. But the beauty was spoilt for me
by something more tangible, the heavy neighbouring presence of a bullet-headed, heavy, middle-aged man, unmis-
takably Prussian. I tried to remember (it becomes increasingly difficult to do so these days) that Burke had said you
could not indict a whole people. Maybe this was a nice German, though appearances were unquestionably against him.
So was the smell of his big cigar, which polluted the crystal
Mediterranean air.

The German had been eyeing me and my English news-

paper curiously. He motioned to me with something between imperiousness and hospitality.

"You are American?" he asked.

I nodded.

"I have heard you speak German, and it is easier for me,
so let us speak German. The name is Klugmann; I am a director of the I. G. Farben. You must have heard of it."

"Everyone has, of course," I said; "one of the biggest industrial concerns in Germany."

"I have spent about six weeks in America," he said. "I gave
three lectures at Pasadena, the California Institute of Tech-
nology. Though I knew no English when I came, I gave
three lectures in English, the third without notes. The students said they understood them. I did it by means of a pho-
netic dictionary. We are very systematic, we Germans."

"It is a well-known German virtue," I said.

"I may as well tell you at once," he said, "I do not approve
of your country. I am sorry, but I do not. I do not approve
of it at all."

"Many Americans do not approve of it completely," I
said, "though we are not so thorough-going. There are lots
of things we Americans do not approve of in our own country. One of the things we do approve of, though, is that we
are allowed to say so publicly, in print and by word of
mouth. Now in the *Nation* here" (my copy had just come),
"for instance, there's a lot about America that you would
agree with. But what do you disapprove of particularly?"

"Well, the waste of natural resources, for one thing. I rode
through the flood areas. It's really shocking. Pure selfishness;
capitalistic greed is responsible. Cutting away a whole tim-
berland just for private greed. The grandchildren of this

generation of Americans will not be grateful to their grand-parents, let me assure you."

"There are other countries," I interrupted, "where the same might be said."

He turned to his wife, who sat silently at his side, and asked her to go to their room and get him another cigar.

"You mean Germany, perhaps. But let me tell you, to understand Germany one must place in the first rank the fact that Personal Egoism has been abolished. Private selfishness, materialism: these have ruined your country; they are re-sponsible for all your troubles. And even with all the won-derful resources you have, so long as Materialism and Egoism are allowed to persist, you are doomed. Now in Germany for the last five years, since the beginning of the Nazi regime, Personal Egoism has been abolished. The individual must realize that first and foremost he is a member of the State, that the State's well-being comes first. That is the great lesson our Führer has taught our people. That is what children are taught in the schools, what they learn in their pre-military service, what people learn in the compulsory labour camps, what I tell our workingmen every day. . . . And you see how well everything goes with us now; everyone is better off; my company has never been more prosperous." He smiled with benevolent satisfaction.

"And is not the Austrian news wonderful?" he asked. "Notice, sir, not a drop of blood spilt. One nation, one people, one Reich. It is *glänzend*."

"Perhaps the Austrians do not think so," I suggested. "There were a million workingmen's signatures just a few weeks ago asking Schuschnigg to count on them to preserve Austrian independence."

"Nonsense. Business brings me often to Austria. Why, do you know, once last year I was at Salzburg, sitting in a café. The waiter leaned over and showed me a Nazi newspaper in his pocket. He said he would be imprisoned if he were seen carrying that. One of his colleagues had been hanged last year for little more."

"We seem to hear that people's heads are cut off in Germany for carrying Marxist literature," I said, "or even expressing liberal democratic sentiments. Indeed, I understand no criticism whatsoever is allowed."

"Lies," he said. "We know in what sort of circles such lies originate. *Responsible* criticism is, of course, allowed. But all the treachery of the democratic regime, that is abolished. We're through with all that. We are a united people, and the Führer will see to it that we stay united. I tell you, the lies about Germany in the foreign press must cease. I used to subscribe to the New York *Times Current History*, but I wrote to the editor three times telling him he must stop lying or I should cancel my subscription."

"It isn't owned by the New York *Times* any more," I interrupted.

"Then by other Jews," he said.

"And now," I said, "you rely for your news about Germany only on the government-controlled press."

Herr Klugmann smiled indulgently. "Of course that is not necessary," he said. "If one wishes to, one can tune in any time one pleases on the radio from Strasbourg. One does not do it for more than five minutes. One hears at once that it is all lies and one is bored. I can assure you, sir, as an industrialist, that everything goes beautifully in our country now, like clockwork; and it will go that way in Austria. You shall see."

"Not for the Jews, surely," I said, "or for the Communists, or for the Austrian nationalists, of whom until just the other day there seemed to be a good many."

"Pure propaganda," he said. "And as for the Jews, of course we've cleared up that matter. That is more than you have done about your Negro problem."

"Is everybody in Germany as satisfied as you are?" I asked.

"But of course. You must not think that it is among the rich and the intelligent alone, or chiefly, that Hitler finds support. His biggest support, I can assure you, comes from the ignorant and the uninformed. I see my workingmen every day and you should hear when they talk with me; their enthusiasm knows no bounds. . . . And why not? Have you heard about our new automobile roads and the Strength through Joy organizations? Our material progress has never been so great or so fast."

"But how about spiritual progress?" I asked. "Fifteen years ago—five years ago—the world was filled with praise for German literature and drama and music and theatre and scholarship. One hears little along that line now. Most of your living writers are in exile, and your scholars and scientists, too. I have met many of them in New York. Einstein, for instance."

"Einstein's conduct is a disgrace," he said. "As for literature and philosophy, et cetera, I confess I am too busy in my business for that sort of thing. But genius is after all a gift from Heaven. It is not our fault that we have none at present. And those exiles you speak of, they were not really geniuses, and of course most of them were Jews, not Germans. Genius, I tell you, is a *Himmelsgeschenk*."

"You got rid of those Heaven gave you," I said.

His wife returned with a cigar. She sat down beside him and looked patient with the patience of one who had heard her husband's exposition of Germanic political principles many times before.

"As for music, in that realm I can speak," he said, lighting his cigar. "We subscribe to the concerts and opera at home. And, would you believe it, in our city there are at least two premières a week, by order? But the musical people will not go to them; they say they prefer Bach and Beethoven. And there seem to be new books published, but I cannot make people out—they prefer to read the old."

"And as for the universities," I said, "can those flourish when no possible freedom of thinking and expression is allowed?"

He laughed uproariously. "How about the Monkey Trial, the evolution case in Tennessee?"

I blushed. I tried to explain that that was quite exceptional, and happened in a backward State, and that such things didn't generally happen in American universities.

"Ach, but they do," he said. "I have read a book by Dr. Flexner, which I found in America. It tells the truth about American universities. You give a doctor's degree in cooking, do you not? With us cooking is women's business; we do not give degrees for it in the universities. And there are other things Flexner tells about. Our government would never allow that book to appear in Germany; it would give too bad an impression of a friendly nation. But such things as you allow to be printed about us; it is scandalous!"

"About concentration camps, you mean," I said, "and purges, and persecution of the Jews and liberals, and the nonsense that is taught as racial science? Are those the things you mean?"

A little later in the day I talked with the elderly German couple who had, among other things, told me bitterly the day before that the most consoling thing about being old in Germany now was that death was so near to look forward to.

"We saw you talking to the Herr Direktor of the I. G.," he said. "We were going to introduce you to him. But we thought you would find him unbearable. Yet I said to my wife: 'No, he must meet him; then he will see what we have to live with daily. After all, he need never see him again.' "

"Does the Herr Direktor believe all he says?" I asked.

"I don't know. I think so. He is a little too one-hundred-and-ten percent. I could tell it to you all by heart; we hear it so much and I am afraid we will, until we die. And you in the democratic countries must beware; this sort of thing is a poison that is spreading in the world, and among the learned in the universities too! Professors in Germany are talking dangerous nonsense now; I trust it won't be contagious!"

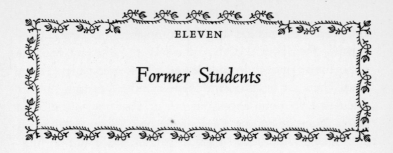

ELEVEN

Former Students

O NCE at a gathering in New York various people were
mentioned who in diverse ways had begun to make
their young presence felt in the world. One had written a
play; another had become a psycho-analyst; still another a
distinguished literary critic; one a radical editor; still another
a foreign correspondent; and one even "the Iron Man" of
big-league baseball. Every once in a while I found myself
murmuring with not greatly concealed pride: "He is a former
student of mine." Finally, a rather bored young lady looked
at me pointedly. "Tell me," she asked, "was Chaliapin a
former student of yours?"

I have since tried, not very successfully, to refrain from
muttering proudly when the brighter young minds among
contemporaries are mentioned: "Former student of mine!"
For I cannot pretend to have taught any of them their present
accomplishments. They did not learn playwriting, psychi-
atry, literary criticism, foreign correspondence, or baseball
from me. And if I were honest, I should have to claim as
former students of mine the hundreds of boring and unpleas-

ant people, the failures and the complacent, successful non-
entities, the rakes and the time-servers, whom I had the
opportunity once to lecture to and whose quiz papers I once
read. There are ten thousand former students of mine, I have
calculated, roaming about the world. That does not include
half a dozen, including some of the best, I have outlived. It
does include hundreds I have forgotten and doubtless hundreds who have forgotten me. I met one of the latter once.
It was at a club in New York. He was a little drunk, and he
looked at me vaguely. He seemed to recall that he had seen
me somewhere. A light dawned.

"I greatly enjoyed that course of yours in—in history."

"Mathematics," I corrected him gently.

"That's it," he said, "mathematics. You made calculus
interesting, I must say."

"No," I said, "it was the theory of functions." I thought
I might as well be credited with something even more majestic that I knew nothing about.

I must admit former students generally do better than that,
and they greet a former teacher with a touching sense that
once long ago they did get something from him. Sometimes
it is nothing more than a joke, used to illustrate something
they have completely forgotten. But the joke remains, and
probably the theory it was meant to illustrate is dated by
now, anyway. Sometimes they surprise you by remembering a quite incidental remark. Occasionally it is good enough
for you to wish you could be sure you *had* said it and they
had not heard it from some other professor—a professor of
calculus, for instance. Or they remember some trick of ges-
ture you had, or the way you suddenly, for emphasis, write
a single word on the blackboard, or the mordant things you

try to say to listeners, cruelties invariably regarded as merely gently whimsical. Or they even remember ideas that, being the first time they had heard them, made a great impression. They are ideas, often, about which by this time you have changed your mind, or lost faith in. One former student told me he had still the notebook he kept in the first year I taught anybody. He promises not to use it for blackmail against me. He insists that I misspelt Malebranche on the blackboard and, as a result, he has misspelt it almost automatically ever since.

Among the students one does remember, there is a tendency to remember them as they were, as, with notebooks before them, they sat as young men of nineteen or twenty in your classroom, or talked with you in your office. I find it hard to realize that time passes, or to realize that though freshmen and sophomores always look the same each year, they don't look the same (though they often are) ten years or fifteen years later. Meeting some of them after a lapse of years, one wonders what has happened to them, or whether one could ever have taught them anything, or where they can have learned all they seem to have found out about books and life, or how they could, who had once been so eager and bright, be so stodgy now.

I have had them look at me, too, in obvious wonder that they could ever have believed I could teach them anything and, once or twice, frankly express resentment at what they had learned.

I often wonder what students remember of a "former teacher," and can judge of their memories only by my own. But I wonder, too, what it is that one teaches them; how much difference a teacher can make. The psycho-analysts assure us these days that the great damage we call education is done largely in the first six years of a child's life, and that a teacher can do less and less fundamentally to the mind and character of a pupil after that as he passes from grade school to college. I hope that is so. It appears to relieve many of us of great responsibilities. The freshman comes with a kind of fatal predestination; he is what he is, and a course or a seminar cannot make any very great difference. I realize how momentary a tangent any teaching is upon a student's psyche, or his mental equipment.

Yet it is something, and something for which students, doubtless with justice, are not grateful.

"Teaching," Santayana writes in *Character and Opinion in the United States,* "is a delightful paternal art, and especially teaching intelligent and warm-hearted youngsters, as most American collegians are; but it is an art like acting, where the performance, often rehearsed, must be adapted to an audience hearing it only once. The speaker must make concessions to their impatience, their taste, their capacity, their prejudices, their ultimate good; he must neither bore nor perplex nor demoralize them. His thoughts must be such as can flow daily, and be set down in notes; they must come when the bell rings and stop appropriately when the bell rings a second time. The best that is in him, as Mephistopheles says in *Faust,* he dare not tell them; and as the substance of this possession is spiritual, to withhold is often to lose it."

What boredom, perplexity, and demoralization do one's students remember! I once caught a glimpse of what it was. I ran into a former student at a week-end in the country. I had known him fairly well and, even before I knew him, had noticed, as had some colleagues, the sharp, critical eye which he fixed upon one during a lecture. There are always half a dozen students in a class in whose presence one would not willingly be boring or stupid or inaccurate. When one is so unwillingly, one sees the immediate register of disappointment (or is it fulfilled expectation?) in their eyes. S—— had been one of those.

The conversation had been general and desultory. At the end of the evening he came into my room. He sat down on a chair and looked at me sharply. He seemed older than he had been, but he had always seemed grown up. He had, I had heard, had various reasons for discouragement, both personal and professional, since he had left college. At one point some years ago he had suddenly turned up and asked if I couldn't think of a good reason for his not committing suicide, since he was about to do so. My reasons were not too good, but they seemed good enough. He was here still, not much happier apparently.

"Look here," he said, "I have been wanting to tell you for some years that your former students have a lot to hold against you, especially the good ones, those who got what you gave them."

"What harm did I do?" I asked, weakly. "I am in a worse case than Socrates. At least he could boast at his trial that none of his former students—those whom he was supposed to have corrupted—had appeared to testify against him. But here you come yourself, saying I have done you irreparable damage. Really, a course in the Philosophy of Art can't do that much harm to anyone, not even to those who get an A."

"Yes it can, and did," he insisted, "and I'm not the only one who was damaged, and you're not the only one who did the damage, though you did a good deal. You taught me

and a good many others to think that contemplation, detachment, eternal things, that Truth, Goodness, and Beauty,
were the proper preoccupations for a young man in this
world. Well, that isn't the kind of world we are living in,
and you gave us a profound sense of unreality. It's taken me
years to get over it and I'm not quite over it yet. But Freud
and Marx have helped me, and I wish I had found out about
them sooner. I must admit I first heard about them from you,
but you didn't sound as if you thought them as important as
Plato or Santayana. You made me live beyond my intellectual income; you made me set store by a lot of things that
had no more relation to the moving things in the world and
to the lives of men than backgammon or Venetian brocades.
I admit you woke me up to a few beautiful things and moving ideas, but it was a fool's Paradise. I've reversed the usual
order and gone through Purgatory since."

"Well, you've found a new Paradise of your own—the
revolution—haven't you?"

"Call it that, but it's one of the forces going on in the
world; it isn't the lost causes of sweetness and light."

I tried to say something about the lost causes being the
only enduring ones; but S—— suddenly softened a little. "It
was a pleasant enough trance while it lasted," he said.

"I'm sorry the coming to was so bad," I said.

Former students are not often so bitter, I must admit. They
are frequently almost embarrassing in their assertion that you
awakened them to think, or to think clearly, or to feel qualities in things and ideas and people they had never perceived
before. They can be incredibly kind, even or especially when
they think they are being objective and just. For it is difficult

to distinguish the persons from the things they communicate, and many a teacher gets a certain glamour in a student's memory because the teacher is associated with that student's first encounter with Plato or Shakespeare, Bach or Phidias. A teacher dealing with great things cannot help sometimes seeming—if only to the undistinguishing young—to be their voice or their oracle; and to a very young mind, if only for a short time, the teacher is confused with the things taught. This may, indeed, be very bad for the teacher, who, in the mirror of his student's generosity, makes something like the same identification, too. His colleagues will correct him, and many of his unbemused students would, too, given the opportunity. For even the luckiest teacher dealing with students avid for ideas will have a good many who look at him as if they dared him to teach them anything. I met one of that category once. He looked at me curiously. "I never could understand," he said, "why you thought philosophy interesting. And yet you seemed to do so. I was quite struck with that fact. That's the only thing I remember from the course."

It should really be a most discouraging fact (I am convinced it is a fact, in any case) that there is nothing much one does for the good student, and nothing very much that one can do for the poor one. In the case of the brilliant successes among former students of mine, I am convinced they were in essence as sophomores what they are now. If they are now learned men, they were already on the road to learning in their sophomore year. One of my former pupils can lay claim now to an erudition that I shall never have. But he was an erudite sophomore, and a little disturbing to an instructor in his first year of teaching. Another, though he is wiser about the world now, was wiser then than I shall ever be about it, and wrote almost as clearly and well then as he does now. The campus politicians are now real politicians, some of them, and not only in the field of politics. Sometimes there are apparent changes: the æsthetes become hardboiled or disillusioned; the sentimentalists, cynics. But even in those cases the change is not always a real one.

Now that I have been teaching more than twenty years and have thus seen five generations—a college generation being four years—of college students, former students seem to return. I do not mean that they come back in the flesh as one did recently with his ten-year-old child to the campus; I mean one recognizes in the sophomore or junior there in the first row a replica of some predecessor not so very different of classes long ago. If I had known fewer students I should have been readier to predict what will become of them. It is easy enough with the run of the mill, though even with them, so rapidly is our world changing, it is not so easy as it used to be. There are not so many fathers' businesses to go into; the typical pre-lawyer may not find an office to be a lawyer in; the young snob and richling may find the world in which he can be both of those things vanishing under his feet. It is not easy even with the "originals," who also, for a teacher long in harness, fall into types. How was I to guess —how would anyone have guessed—that the editor of the best college humorous magazine in ten years, neatly ironic, merrily sceptical, and amusedly disillusioned, would turn into an uncompromising revolutionary, the Washington correspondent of the *Daily Worker?* How was one to suspect that the playboy whose life was bounded by fraternities and dances and drinking would be sobered by something or other into becoming a diligent professional classical scholar—a pedantic one at that? How could I have dreamed (though I might have done so) that the withering cynic of his class, whose god was Swift, should have become a mystical and fanatical rabbi?

I suspect that in each of these cases, had I been wiser or known my student better, I should not have had much occasion for surprise. There is much one does not find out about students, since it is natural that a teacher does rather more of the talking. And there is a lot one would never find out from the way in which students talk to a teacher.

There is only one thing by which I continue, with a foolish and persistent naïveté, to be surprised. I expect, somehow, that a student ten years after college will still have the brightness and enthusiasm, the disinterested love of ideas, and the impersonal passion for them that some develop during their undergraduate days. Time and again I have run into them, and wondered what the world has done to them that that passionate detachment should have gone. I know some of the things, brutal or familiar enough to the point almost of banality: a family, the struggle for a living, a disillusion with the status of contemplation in the nightmare of a violent world. But it is not revolution or disillusion that surprises me; both are intelligible. It is the death-in-life that assails the spirits of young men who had been alive when I knew them at college. A fierce hate, a transcendent revolutionary contempt for ideas, especially traditional ones, a revolt against the academy; all these things are not dismaying. They are symptoms that life is not dead and that spirit lives in some form, however tortured or fantastic or unprecedented. It is when spirit is utterly dead, when the one-time eager youth becomes precociously middle-aged, that one feels above all that education is a failure. One awakened something for a short time. But did one? Perhaps I have, like a good many teachers, flattered myself. It was not we who awakened them; it was the season of their lives, and the things and ideas which, despite us, for a moment—if only for a moment—stirred them. There are times when, if one thought about former students too much, one could not go on teaching. For the teacher meeting his former students is reminded of the fact that Plato long ago pointed out in the *Republic*. It is not what the teacher but what the world teaches them that will in the long run count, and what they can learn from the latter comes from habits fixed soon after birth and temperaments fixed long before it. There are just a few things a teacher can do, and that only for the sensitive and the spirited. He can initiate enthusiasms, clear paths, and inculcate discipline. He can communicate a passion and a method; no more. His most serious triumph as a teacher is the paradoxical one of having his students, while he is teaching them and perhaps afterwards, forget him in the absorption of the tradition or the inquiry of which he is the transient voice. Lucky for him if later his students feel his voice was just. As in the playing of music, it is the music, not the musician, that is ultimate. And in the art of teaching, it is what is taught that counts, not the teacher. It is a great tribute to an artist to say that he plays Beethoven or Bach, and puts nothing between them and his audience. But in so doing he becomes one with both the composer and the listener. In the listener's memory he anonymously shares the composer's immortality. The teacher, too, is best remembered who is thus forgotten. He lives in what has happened to the minds of his students, and in what they remember of things infinitely greater than themselves or than himself. They will remember, perhaps, that once in a way, in the midst of the routine of the classroom, it was something not himself that spoke, something not themselves that listened. The teacher may well be content to be otherwise forgotten, or to live in something grown to ripeness in his students that he, however minutely, helped bring to birth. There are many students thus come to fruition whom I should be proud to have say: "He was my teacher." There is no other immortality a teacher can have.

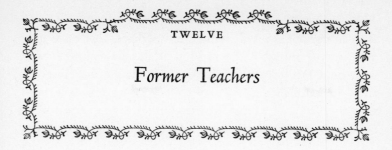

TWELVE

Former Teachers

BY AN easy transition I am led from reflection about former students to meditation on former teachers. For I
have had teachers as well as pupils, and in considering what
effect one has had, or failed to have, on one's one-time students, I cannot help looking back on teachers who, though
they might be embarrassed to acknowledge it, or insistent on
denying it, had an influence over me. I shall leave out my
early love for Miss Foley in 4A, or Miss Carpendale in 7B,
whom I feared horribly, partly because she taught me the
impossible subject of arithmetic, and partly because of her
immense height and blazing red hair and unrelenting expression and deep mannish voice. I felt rather sorry for the trim
little teacher of shopwork (another impossible subject) when
I heard Miss Carpendale had married him. I was sure even
then that that was the way it had happened.

I shall begin rather with high school, for I don't remember
that in grade school anybody aroused my mind and imagination. That event came in my first term at Townsend
Harris Hall, the preparatory school, called at the time the

academic department, of the College of the City of New
York. The man involved was named Michael J. Kelleher, an
enthusiastic, curly-haired Irishman, who, at the top of his
voice but with a winning cadence, dragooned us into liking
The Ancient Mariner and *Ivanhoe*. He also dragooned some of
us into liking our own writing. He was the first one, save,
perhaps, Miss Foley, to make me think I could write. Miss
Foley's observation had been based on one sentence. I had
written a self-portrait of a camel. The last sentence was: "I
do not need water for days at a time; I have it with me." She
said that was very good and very well informed. Mr. Michael
Kelleher wrote in a large bold hand on a theme of mine:
"This has the sweet breath of the country about it." It was an
essay on Central Park.

But I recall Mr. Michael Kelleher chiefly because he gave
us the contagious impression of so liking poetry that he
simply had to tell us about it. Since we were the fourth class
he had each morning, it occurred to me even then that it was
very remarkable that he should be able to care so deeply and
vividly about Rebecca and Rowena still. But he did. It was,
I found out, the first year he had taught. I have often thought
since it might be well to have a big turn-over in the teaching
profession. But that is not really necessary. For, years later,
finding myself in the neighbourhood of my old school, I decided to hunt out my old teacher. It was not quite the end
of the hour and I heard the powerful cadenced voice of Mr.
Kelleher still making clear to fourteen-year-olds the wonder
and mystery of *The Ancient Mariner*. I could hear him and
even see his figure outlined through the transparent glass of
the door:

> *"Alone, alone, all, all alone,*
> *Alone on a wide, wide sea,*
> *And never a saint took pity on*
> *My soul in agony . . ."*

The remembered shiver went up my spine. Mr. Kelleher was a born teacher of poetry. He did not explain it; he communicated it by contagion.

There were three other high school teachers I remember. One was the beautifully dressed, slim Mr. Knickerbocker who taught us French. His technique belied his debonair appearance. There was no languid elegance about his methods. He spent the first fifteen minutes of each hour rapidly going around the class making certain that we knew the new words in each lesson. It was a martinet method, but it worked. One did not twice come to class unprepared, to have Mr. Knickerbocker's clear blue eyes briefly stare one into humiliation if one guessed, or could not even guess, the meaning of a word. There was not much about appreciation of French literature, and I presume such methods now would be regarded as unimaginative drill. But one knew a great many French words with precision before the term was over.

My third debt to my high school teachers is to Bird W. Stair, now a professor in the College of the City of New York. He had just come to New York from Indiana; he used the English class as an introduction to ideas, and I suspect my feeling that literature was the vehicle, sensuous and imaginative, of ideas came from him. After three terms with him I had learned once and for all that books, even old ones, were distillations of life, and began to think less of literature with a capital L. As I look back on it now, I am quite sure that Mr. Stair found Burke's Speech on Conciliation and *Macbeth* the springboards for various ideas that had a rather tenuous connexion with them. "English" became at his hands an introduction to philosophy, manners, contemporary political ideas, journalism, and love. These ideas were not always directly germane to the text; but they were ideas, and though their accent and their origin were Middle-Western—Middle-Western *révolté*—they were an introduction to the great world and to the realm of mind.

The fourth teacher I recall in high school is one who, if he still lives, may possibly remember me. If he does, he recalls me as the worst student of mathematics he ever had. Rumour circulated in the school that Mr. Powell, an urbane, sad man who looked like a banker, was a very wealthy man who taught simply to occupy his time. I never believed it; no one would, I thought, teach solid geometry for amusement. If I were rich, I kept on thinking during the class, I should buy a yacht; I should go around the world. I should, if I must teach, teach English. Mr. Powell noticed my mind wandering; he also noticed when I came up to the blackboard for a demonstration that mathematics was not my *forte*. He called me to him once at the end of the hour. "You do not seem stupid," he said, "but mathematics seems a lot of hocus pocus to you." For the most part, it still does; and I regret it very much. For I am told on good authority that in the logistic symbols of the newer mathematics lies hid the secret of the universe. I recall also that Plato said a gift for mathematics was essential to a philosopher. But it is too late to do anything about it now; it was too late then. And when it came to trigonometry, I, too, was "alone on a wide, wide sea," and Mr. Powell I always remember as the only teacher of mathematics ever to take pity on my soul in agony.

When one speaks of one's old teachers, it is generally to one's college teachers that one refers. For it is then, if one is lucky, that one comes in contact with men who communicate and articulate the things and ideas which become the seeds of one's later intellectual and imaginative life. Every college has five or six men who in essence are its educational system. I was very lucky. For during my undergraduate days at Columbia, there was a galaxy of teachers available to the student who in their respective ways and as a group would be hard to duplicate at any college in any period. As a freshman straight from high school, I heard Charles A. Beard lecture on American Government; as a sophomore—and in 1914—I heard Carlton Hayes lecture on European History; as a junior I heard John Erskine talk on Shakespeare, and was in a small class where he taught us, really taught us, writing; and in my senior year I had the unique and irrecoverable experience of traversing the history of philosophy with Frederick J. E. Woodbridge. It was not until my graduate study that I came to know John Dewey.

Charles A. Beard illustrates something very remarkable about the art of teaching. Today everybody, even the literary youngsters, are interested in government. For even literature seems less in the Ivory Tower than it did in 1913. But the study of government, then officially known at Columbia as "Politics," did not, to most of us addicted to poetry and music, seem to be our meat, and there was nothing in the big dark blue tome, Beard's *American Government and Politics*, that seemed arresting. There were endless details about the mechanisms and structure of State and Federal government. It was not the Beard of the *Economic Interpretation of the Constitution*.

But his lectures were another matter. The lanky figure leaning against the wall, drawling wittily with half-closed eyes, made the questions of government seem the most vital that anyone could broach, and touched matters that lay far deeper than the mere forms of constitutional government.

Every good teacher has his own special art; with some, it is a genius for a clarity that sometimes is more lucid than the complexities of the subject justify. Sometimes it is a talent for apophthegm or leading suggestion, a word that evokes a vista or an idea that opens a world. I cannot now quite remember what Professor Beard's special technique was. He was clear, he was suggestive, he was witty. But none of these things could quite account for the hold he had on the smug and the rebels alike, on both the pre-lawyers and the pre-poets. I suspect it was a certain combination of poetry, philosophy, and honesty in the man himself, a sense he communicated that politics mattered far beyond the realm commonly called political, and an insight he conveyed into the life that forms of government furthered or betrayed. One morning he came into class as usual, stood against the wall, and, half-closing his eyes, said:

"Gentlemen, today we are to discuss the budget system in State government. I am sure that must seem to you a dull subject. But if you will tell me, gentlemen, how much *per capita* a nation spends on its Army, on its Navy, on education, on public works, I shall be able to tell you, I think, as much about that nation as if you gave me the works of its poets and philosophers."

We listened with revised and revived attention to an exposition, full of figures and detail, of the State budget system. Charles A. Beard showed us what politics had to do with the life beyond it and which it made possible. And he taught us, too, the difference between the forms of government and the living substance of its operations. Under his easy, drawling manner, we sensed a passionate concern for an understanding of the realities of government, the economic forces and the interested persons involved in it, and the ideal of government: the liberation of the energies of men. Nobody who has ever listened to Beard can disdain the study of politics in favour of the study of "higher things." He has been too well taught, as tragic world events have since shown, how government may nourish or destroy "higher things."

Up to the autumn of 1914 Europe seemed to most American college students a solar system away. In the autumn of 1914, when the war had been going on two months, Europe came for the first time in the imagination of many Americans to be vivid and near. European history ceased to be the anthropology and archæology of distant peoples who spoke remote languages. It became as alive as yesterday's events: it was what explained today's news. It was, therefore, no wonder that at the beginning of the college year Carlton Hayes's course in "Europe since 1815" had become the most popular course in Columbia College. But it was not only the war that accounted for that. Carlton Hayes had for some time been one of the most popular professors in the college. His lectures were the most famous dramatic spectacle on the campus. Nor was it as a performance alone that they were famous. Everyone had heard that Hayes could actually make clear French political parties; I have never met anybody since who could or can. . . . The complicated history of Germany in the second half of the nineteenth century took shape as well as drama under his presentation of it. And in the midst of being taught and taught clearly, one had the incidental and additional pleasure of hearing a man to whom the great catastrophe of war had its roots in a past he knew, in the traditions of nations among whom he had lived familiarly, and in the desperate mythologies of nationalism, to which he had given special study and concern. One was treated, besides, to unforgettable vignettes of Disraeli dropping his morning walking stick as the cannons boomed noon at Gibraltar; of the Manchester school of economists, the "spiritual advisers" to the robber barons of early nineteenth-century industrial England; of the black walnut furniture of the Victorian period; of the times and the manners of Louis Napoleon; of the studious German Jew in the British Museum whose studies produced the *Communist Manifesto*. One was shaken out of the smugness of the middle-class world in which most students were brought up and out of the provincial Americanism in which most of us had lived.

It did not matter, it served only as spice, that some of the barbs delivered in a dry voice by this baldish, sharp-featured man in his thirties were directed at us, at our very smugness, at our laziness, or at our fathers: when he was explaining the attitude of the manufacturers of the early Industrial Revolution, he reminded us that we all knew manufacturers; "some of your fathers," he drawled, "are manufacturers." It did matter a little to some of us that he mocked poetry and philosophy (this *in re* Shelley and Godwin) . . . "philosophy is what is taught in Philosophy Hall. . . ." But it did not matter much. For during a whole year, we sat through a whole century of European history, and Bismarck, Garibaldi, Social Legislation in England. Benevolent Tories like Shaftesbury and reformers like Cobden and Bright, "nationalism" —what devastating force Carlton Hayes put and can still put into the word—democracy, the Third Republic, became familiar parts of our imagination. In the midst of cries of "pro-German" and "pro-Ally," "preparedness" and "pacifism," during the three years before America went into the war, we knew somewhat better than many of our older compatriots what had brought the tornado about. Carlton Hayes had brought European history, as Charles Beard had brought American government, from the abstraction of a textbook to an experience lived and a problem to be faced. And it always surprised some of us that, in the midst of the lectures— first-rate theatrical performances, words shot out for emphasis, silences sustained for a moment, gestures and movements deployed like those of a good actor—when we looked down at our notes, they were as ordered and clear as if we had listened to a scholastic metronome. . . . I confess with shame that I achieved only a B.

You were allowed, if you had a fairly good academic record, to take in the senior year a graduate course that was at the time one of the famous academic enterprises of the period. It was James Harvey Robinson's course in the History of the Intellectual Classes in Western Europe. Everyone who had gone to high school knew the two volumes of Robinson and Beard's *Development of Modern Europe*. But the Robinson we came to know as a legend and a rumour by the time we were sophomores was the Robinson who had invented the "new history"—the history of causes and consequences, the history that treated politics as the surface of more fundamental matters, economic and social and cultural, and that regarded the date of the invention of the steam engine as more important than the dates of a king, and the industrial use of steam as more significant than monarchies and dynasties. We had also heard of Robinson, along with Dewey and Beard, as among the intellectual-liberal forces that were making our university famous in some quarters, notorious in others. And, finally, we had heard of the remarkable brilliance of the lectures in History 72.

The latter was a graduate course to which undergraduates, a handful of us, were admitted on sufferance. The majority of the class of over two hundred were graduate students of history, many of them women high school teachers from all over the country, particularly the West and South. Professor Robinson was a short man, with thin, greying hair and a deprecating, half-tired, half-amused, drawling voice. He seemed to be having a half-weary good time examining the origins of human stupidity, and those vestigial remains of our culture that blocked the free and hopeful functioning of human intelligence. It took us a few weeks in the course to get to the beginnings of *intellectual* history. For Robinson, with saturnine delight, liked to show us the mind of the child, the slave, and the animal still functioning in us. Once he brought in a leading editorial from the New York *Times* to illustrate the theme, and another time quoted from a batch of Sunday sermons reported in that journal the next day. The course was not a course in intellectual heroes, but a course in the changing fashions of adult follies taken seriously in various ages. It only gradually became clear what intellectual heroes were presiding over the whole story as he gave it. They were Freud and Marx and Dewey and the anthropologists, and H. G. Wells, the prophet, then, of intelligence reshaping the world. There were only two or three gods of the past left unbesmirched, or whose clay feet were not recognized. They were Lucretius, who saw the diabolism of religion; Francis Bacon, who saw the human possibilities of science; Voltaire, who exhibited the foolishness of superstition. Plato was a man who believed in Truth, Goodness, and Beauty because he saw the actual world as a chaos which, Robinson loved to remind us, he compared to "a man with a running nose. . . ." Aristotle's science was childish (Robinson did not know how soon again it was to be fashionable and how more fundamental than fashion it is); St. Augustine was a most amusingly and scandalously human saint. It was not until the enlightenment of the eighteenth century that anybody, so most of us gathered from the course, was very enlightened.

Many of the graduate students were shocked, especially by the treatment of religion. The undergraduates from Columbia College had heard much of this before and had no faith (as did some of the graduate students) to have taken away. One of the young women complained to Professor Robinson: "You are taking away my faith." He looked at her oddly. "But if I took away a headache," he said simply, "you would not complain."

We undergraduates enjoyed the sallies, the freshness, the irreverence, and enjoyed, too, the fundamental feeling that lay at the basis of it all—that man, if he took his own intelligence into his hands—could make the world less a shambles and an idiocy than it had so often been. It was in the great days of the liberal faith when trust in intelligence was in the ascendant. If Robinson made the world appear a satire to intelligent observation, he made it seem a lyric hope to generosity and understanding. Dixon Ryan Fox, now President of Union College, was the young instructor who took the third quiz hour with the undergraduates. He felt it his special obligation to let us see the other side. And after a week, when he knew Robinson had been "exposing" modern Protestantism, he called in the chaplain as a counterweight. He need not have bothered; we had our own grains of salt. One of the reasons we had grains of salt was that some of us had been studying with a man who will go down, I am quite certain, as one of the great philosophical teachers of our generation. His slender published writings will live, but they will live for a small circle of students. But Frederick J. E. Woodbridge has educated a whole generation of students in philosophy; and a whole circle of them scattered over the country, including Morris Cohen and Sidney Hook and J. H. Randall, Jr., and Herbert Schneider (to mention only a few), are living testimonies to his influence and his power. In my college days, the great thing was to have taken his course in the History of Philosophy. Some of us were taking it at the same time that we took Robinson's History of the Intellectual Classes in Western Europe. It was rather a different story we were told. It was not a story, but a succession of experiences of philosophers whose importance lay "not in their truth but in their power." It was a shock that turned into a liberation for those of us who had come to philosophy looking for *the* Truth with a dogmatic capital letter. There were other shocks, too. Much that was said in the textbooks we never heard in class, or we heard the contrary. Professor

Woodbridge, who looked like a bishop and would have made a very eloquent one, talked like a poet whose theme happened to be the human mind. He talked most like a poet on the days when he was most interested; one remembers what days those were: the early Greeks, Plato, Aristotle, Marcus Aurelius, Lucretius, Spinoza with his sovereign detachment, and Locke with his sovereign common sense. He was not an unprejudiced observer and we rather liked the frankness and the brevity with which he dismissed the Germans and Rousseau. But what one was most moved by was the things by which he himself was most moved: the Plato who was the son of Apollo, the poet and the dramatist of ideas; Marcus Aurelius, the disillusioned statesman whistling to keep up his cosmical courage; Lucretius looking out with dramatic sympathy and equable understanding on the eternal nature of things. We were impressed by a mind whose maturity had not dulled its enthusiasms, and an understanding uncorrupted by the technical controversies of the academy, by the routine of the classroom, by the burden of administration of an elder statesman, for Woodbridge was graduate Dean of the University. He taught a whole generation of students of philosophy to keep their eye on the object, to see a thinker in his own terms, to cease to raise foolish and irrelevant questions, and, above all, to raise the central and relevant ones about a man's teaching. On Aristotle's metaphysics, he began by reminding us that Aristotle was asking the simple and the ultimate question: "What does it mean to be? . . ." We found ourselves astonished to be reminded that the Middle Ages were in their own time not the Middle Ages at all. We were made aware of Locke's simple English attempt to be sensible, tolerant, and direct, and learned to understand what Spinoza meant and why he saw it as a liberation to see all things under the form of eternity. For in that wonderful class, as Will Durant (sitting next to me in alphabetical order) remarked, we were listening not to a professor of philosophy but to philosophy itself. It was impossible to feel you were listening to a doctrine; Professor Woodbridge has never founded a school. You were hearing philosophy itself and came to understand it as an attempt to speak in the categories of mind of the categories of things.

I did not—I think not many of us did—understand it all. But we began to understand what understanding meant, in words that had eloquence without rhetoric. We heard great things nobly uttered. We learnt no doctrine but we grasped the significance of intellectual procedure; and to a whole generation of philosophers, though Professor Woodbridge has long since ceased to be their teacher, he remains their teacher still. He made us understand as none else had done, to use one of his own phrases, "the enterprise of learning."

A figure more widely known outside purely academic circles was and is John Dewey. In 1915 his name was already, if not a household, certainly a schoolroom word. His *How We Think* was used in all the normal schools of the country, and even fashionable ladies dipped into his far from easy books. I had read almost all of Dewey I could get hold of by the time I was a senior, but it was not until my first year as a graduate student that I heard, or, I believe, saw him. His familiar figure and speech, seeming at first that of a Vermont farmer, the casual gait, the keen but often absent eyes, seem so familiar now that I can scarcely believe I did not know them before.

I admit the first lecture was quite a shock, a shock of dullness and confusion, if that can be said. It was at any rate a disappointment. I had not found Dewey's prose easy, but I had learned that its difficulty lay for the most part in its intellectual honesty, which led him to qualify an idea in one sentence half a page long. In part also it lay in the fact that this profoundly original philosopher was struggling to find a vocabulary to say what had never been said in philosophy before, to find a diction that would express with exactness the reality of change and novelty, philosophical words having been used for centuries to express the absolute and the fixed. Once one had got used to the long sentences, with their string of qualifying clauses, to the sobriety, to the lack of image and of colour, one sensed the liberating force of this philosophy. Here was not an answer but a quest for light in the living movement of human experience; in the very precariousness of experience there lay open to the perplexed human creature the possibilities that peril itself provocatively suggested. I had found here, as have so many of my generation, a philosophy that, instead of laying down a diagram of an ideal universe that had nothing to do with the one of actual human doings and sufferings, opened a vision of conscious control of life, of a democracy operating through creative intelligence in the liberation of human capacities and natural goods. In *How We Think* I had learned that thinking itself was simply a discipline of the animal habit of trial and error, and of the possible human habit of imagination and foresight. In *Democracy and Education* I had gathered that it was not in the forms of democratic government that true democracy lay, but in the substance of intelligent co-operation, largely dependent on education. Dewey was not easy, but once one had mastered his syntax, a vision of a liberal and liberated commonwealth was one's reward, and a philosophy that was not only a vision but a challenge.

I was naturally prepared, therefore, to expect something of intellectual excitement from the lectures in "Psychological Ethics." Intellectual excitement was the last term to describe what I experienced that September afternoon. The course came, in the first place, directly after lunch. It was well attended; there were even some fashionably dressed society ladies, for Dewey had become a vogue. But this famous philosopher who had written so much on "Interest in Education," as the essence of the educational process, could not, save by a radical distortion of the term, be said at first hearing to sound interesting. He had none of the usual tricks or gifts of the effective lecturer. He sat at his desk, fumbling with a few crumpled yellow sheets and looking abstractedly out of the window. He spoke very slowly in a Vermont drawl. He looked both very kindly and very abstracted. He hardly seemed aware of the presence of a class. He took little pains to underline a phrase, or emphasize a point, or, so at first it seemed to me, to make any. Occasionally he would apparently realize that people in the back of the room might not hear his quiet voice; he would then accent the next word, as likely as not a preposition or a conjunction. He seemed to be saying whatever came into his head next, and at one o'clock on an autumn afternoon to at least one undergraduate what came next did not always have or seem to have a very clear connexion with what had just gone before. The end of the hour finally came and he simply stopped; it seemed to me he might have stopped anywhere. But I soon found that it was my mind that had wandered, not John Dewey's. I began very soon to do what I had seldom done in college courses—to take notes. It was then a remarkable discovery to make on looking over my notes to find that what had seemed so casual, so rambling, so unexciting, was of an extraordinary coherence, texture, and brilliance. I had been listening not to the semi-theatrical repetition of a discourse many times made—a fairly accurate description of many academic lectures—I had been listening to a man actually *thinking* in the presence of a class. As one became accustomed to Dewey's technique, it was this last aspect of his teaching that was most impressive—and educative. To attend a lecture of John Dewey was to participate in the actual business of thought. Those pauses were delays in creative thinking, when the next step was really being considered, and for the glib dramatics of the teacher-actor was substituted the enterprise, careful and candid, of the genuine thinker. Those hours came to seem the most arresting educational experiences, almost, I have ever had. One had to be scrupulously attentive and one learned to be so. Not every day or in every teacher does one overhear the palpable processes of thought. One came to enjoy and appreciate the homely metaphor, "the fork in the road," the child and his first attempts to speak, the New England town meeting, instead of the classical images one had been accustomed to from more obviously eloquent lips. Moreover, if one listened attentively one discovered apophthegm and epigram delivered as casually and sleepily as if they were clichés. I remember one instance. It had been rather a long lecture designed to show that the crucial tests of the morals of a group came in what that group regarded as violations of its conventions. The bell rang. Professor Dewey began to crumple up his notes. "And so," he said, "I think sometimes one can tell more about the morals of our society from the inmates of its jails than from the inmates of its universities." The student next to me who had been semi-dozing stirred in half-alarmed surprise.

I learned later in a seminar to see Dewey's greatest gifts as a teacher, that of initiating inquiry rather than that of disseminating a doctrine. The subject matter of the seminar was innocent enough and removed from the immediacies of current controversy. It was a year's course, meeting every Tuesday afternoon, on "The Logic of John Stuart Mill." The seminar remains in my memory, it must be added, not simply for John Dewey or John Stuart Mill. It consisted, looking back on it and indeed as it appeared then, of a very remarkable group. It included two now well-known professors of philosophy, Brand Blanshard of Swarthmore College and Sterling Lamprecht of Amherst, Paul Blanshard, later to become Commissioner of Accounts under Mayor La Guardia, and Albert C. Barnes, the inventor and manufacturer of Argyrol and collector of French paintings, even then a grey-haired man who used to come up from Philadelphia every week with his secretary expressly to study philosophy with his friend John Dewey.

I don't suppose Professor Dewey said more than five percent of the words actually uttered in that seminar. For the latter consisted largely of papers presented by various members of the group. But one remembered what he said. The subject matter was obviously close to him, for had not Mill been one of the great nineteenth-century leaders of the empirical school of thought; had he not been, in his way, a pragmatist and, like Dewey himself, a liberal? But one notices particularly Dewey's gift for pointing to the exact difficulty or the exact limitations of a man or a paper; his capacity for sympathetically seeing what a student was driving at, even when he did not quite succeed in saying it, and Dewey's candid expression of his own position or his own prejudices.

One instance of Dewey's frankness comes to my mind. There was among the group a young lady who had come from England where she had studied philosophy with Bertrand Russell at Cambridge. She listened patiently for weeks to Dewey's varied insistence that the truth of an idea was tested by its use. One day she burst out toward the close of the seminar in the sharp, clipped speech of the educated Englishwoman: "But, professor, I have been taught to believe that true means true; that false means false, that good means good and bad means bad; I don't understand all this talk about more or less true, more or less good. Could you explain more exactly?"

Professor Dewey looked at her mildly for a moment and said: "Let me tell you a parable. Once upon a time in Philadelphia there was a paranoiac. He thought he was dead. Nobody could convince him he was alive. Finally, one of the doctors thought of an ingenious idea. He pricked the patient's finger. 'Now,' he said, 'are you dead?' 'Sure,' said the paranoiac, 'that proves that dead men bleed. . . .' Now I'll say true or false if you want me to, but I'll mean better or worse."

There are all kinds of talents that go to make up a great teacher. Among those not commonly noted in the textbooks are simplicity and candour. These qualities in Dewey even an undergraduate could recognize and understand.

I cannot say that John Erskine seemed to me a great man in the sense that Woodbridge and Dewey did and do, nor

did *The Private Life of Helen of Troy,* for all its bright enter-
tainment, lead me to think I had been obtuse on this point
as an undergraduate. But I am convinced he was a very remarkable teacher and it has always seemed to me a pity that
he gave up the profession of distinguished teaching for that
of the popular novelist. Erskine's quality as a teacher was
that of communication by contagion; you felt the quality
of the authors he talked about and books seemed to have
something to do with life rather than libraries.

Literature was an exercise in imagination, not in archæology and there must be thousands of students besides myself
who learned to read authors in their own terms, to enjoy
them for their own sakes, from John Erskine's famous course
in Elizabethan Literature. It is true that one enjoyed Professor Erskine for other reasons. He had wit—often malicious—
in his own right, and, when he was in the vein, poetry and
philosophy, too. He obviously loved poetry and it seemed
to him both to matter and a matter of course that we should
love it, too. One felt about him something of the prima
donna lecturer; it was evidenced by the pointed silence that
would occur while some unfortunate late-comer found his
way to his seat. It was clear, too, from the way in which, not
infrequently, Shakespeare or Marlowe or Castiglione would
be the springboards for little bravura lectures by our teacher
on the importance of love or of being a cultivated gentleman, the latter one of his favourite themes. But if he was
sometimes the prima donna, he always respected the materials he taught, and for many years no one at Columbia was a
more devoted servant to the art and to the love of literature
than he. And not the least of his services to that art were,
first, the noble and musical way in which he read poetry it-

self; and, secondly, the pains he took to encourage signs of that art among undergraduates. Other teachers might make literature seem a set of documents to be investigated; no one quite knew why. Erskine made it an art to be lived and loved.

It is occasionally said that a good student needs no teachers and that all that he does need is a library and leisure. Neither the poor nor the good student needs bad teachers or bored ones; he is better off without them. But he is very fortunate indeed if he can look back on his college days and enumerate half a dozen men who, by their passion for ideas, their clarity about them, their love for the communication of them, their exemplification in their own being of intellectual discipline and candour, have given a meaning to facts that, even with leisure and libraries, he would not have been as likely to find by himself.

I feel my college generation at Columbia was very fortunate. Half a dozen good teachers in a college are enough to make it distinguished. We had more than half a dozen very exceptional ones. But then I think current undergraduates at Columbia, if they are discerning, will, looking back, be able to say the same.

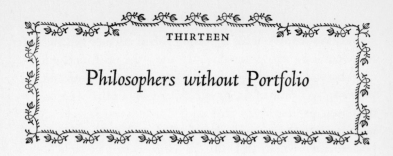

THIRTEEN

Philosophers without Portfolio

I HAVE often observed an embarrassed confusion in the lay mind as to just what it is that one teaches when one teaches philosophy. Nobody would look blank if you told him you taught chemistry or history or mathematics. But time and again when, being asked what I teach, I have replied philosophy, the questioner has looked or expressed his bewilderment. I have given up explaining, partly because the more one thinks about it the more one wonders what, after all, *is* philosophy. One cannot find agreement, certainly among one's professional colleagues. But that is not why I have given up explaining. The reason is rather that just when I think I have made everything clear, it turns out that the questioner usually has his own idea of what philosophy is, a notion which he has been waiting patiently to explain. Usually the explanation begins with: "I have a kind of philosophy myself." The latter turns out generally to be some version, very much watered down, of Robert Ingersoll or Mary Baker Eddy.

The fact is, however, that the layman is instinctively

sound. He knows what a distinguished former teacher of my own long ago pointed out to me—the profound difference between being a philosopher and being a professor of philosophy. Some of the greatest philosophers have certainly not been professors of philosophy or of anything else. Spinoza is a notable example; he even refused the chance, it will be remembered, to teach at the University of Heidelberg. On the other hand, it is possible, even likely, that one will "teach" philosophy without acquiring the philosophical habit of mind. For, after all, what is philosophy but an attempt, as Matthew Arnold said of Sophocles, "to see life steadily and see it whole," to have a total and consistent point of view toward nature and destiny? It is not necessary to draw a salary for doing that in order to do it, nor, having such a perspective, to teach it to students or to teach other philosophers' points of view to them, Monday, Wednesday, and Friday at eleven. If a philosopher must teach, as it was once suggested, it might be better if he taught something else than philosophy. It might be best if he did not teach at all and took instead an easy job taking in the umbrellas in a museum. For in the classroom one's ideas harden into doctrines, one's insights into routines, one's doubts coagulate into neat, expoundable pseudo-clarities. As I recall philosophers I have known from earliest childhood, not all of them have had portfolios; they have not been officially certificated as thinkers in academies. They have been men and women, sometimes in obscure walks of life, sometimes men of action whom a just and candid observation of their experience, and reflection upon it, have led to an ultimate and residual point of view upon existence. They have not always known the books of the learned, or when they have known them, it is not from those, or primarily from those, that their philosophies or their insights have come.

There is indeed a good deal to be said against the modern habit of segregating "philosophers" as a special group attached to universities. The business of making things clear and making them vivid to adolescents is not necessarily, or perhaps at all, the way to arrive at a considered way of life or attitude toward nature. Teaching breeds the habit of thinking in terms that have a specious lucidity or a dangerous winsomeness or credibility. Moving in "professional" philosophical circles nourishes the tendency, moreover, to become involved in the technique of controversy for its own sake, to become calloused to, negligent of, what Plato called the "great business itself." The amateur philosopher outside the academy may often be loose, and frequently inept, but he will, if he has anything of "philosophy" in him, keep to essential issues in philosophy, the only ones there are, and ultimate things; in philosophy there should be no others.

I like to recall the men and women I have known who, without any professional connexion with academic philosophy, none the less felt themselves driven to arrive at some fundamental attitude toward life and the world, to make their peace with first and last things. The elderly brother and sister in the country radio shop in Vermont, Emersonians without knowing it; the Federal judge; the retired jewellery manufacturer who had thought his way to content; the Sicilian peasant who had found a path to fortitude; the Colorado school auditor; the tuberculosis specialist; the one-time Javanese civil servant in Amsterdam; Mathilde, the elevator operator in Philosophy Hall; and Maria, who takes care of my apartment and of me.

All such "philosophers despite themselves," however, must be sharply distinguished from the many persons—there must be thousands of them in the United States—who try, usually with pathetic maladroitness, to be non-official experts in philosophy. Every professional teacher of philosophy knows, as a matter of fact, that America, so much given over (according to foreign observers) to materialism and practicality, nourishes an extraordinary number of private persons who set store by a philosophical system, elaborate, technical-sounding, long-winded, which they have formulated in the intervals or at the close of a practical life. There must be almost as many people with unpublished philosophies as there are obscure citizens with unproduced plays in their attics or their trunks. Every year at the university I meet or hear from some of these. Usually it is some business man who in the midst of acquiring a fortune, or often having consolidated or perhaps lost one, has had light in his bonnet the bee of formulating a System of Nature, of Life, of Thought. . . .

There was, for example, Mr. R——. One morning there appeared in my office a jolly, chubby, red-faced little man, his bald head gleaming brightly. He carried a large briefcase under his arm. He had been in the toy manufacturing business all his life, he explained, but in the intervals he had begun to work out a system of cosmology. He had never had time to read the professional philosophers much, and when he did, he had not made too much out of them, and they seemed to him, moreover, the victims of their own vocabularies. But he had thought systematically about life and the world, and he had evolved a system. Here it was. He opened his briefcase and placed a huge typewritten manuscript on my desk. He had sent it to various publishers but nobody seemed in-

terested. He had sent it all the way to France to Bergson. He
had had a polite note in return, but Bergson was apparently
not very well and was very busy. He knew I was busy, too,
but I looked well enough, and I must certainly not be as busy
as Bergson. He was quite sure he had solved some of the
great puzzles of the universe. And there was a practical side
to it, too. The reason there was so much chaos in the world
was that the Method of Direct Reasonableness had never
been applied to human problems. Now in his system . . .
would I read it and tell him whether I thought there was anything in it? It was terribly hard to break through the professional crust, the closed shop of the philosophers. It was only
five hundred pages, and he had been working on it, on and
off, especially through slack periods in the toy business, for
forty years. Perhaps he had hit upon things that the professionals had remained blind to. He would be ever so much
obliged.

Five hundred pages of manuscript was not a pleasure to be
looked forward to at the moment, even with the off chance
that the great puzzles had all been resolved. It was the season
of the year when I was besieged with term papers and Ph.D.
dissertations. But my amateur philosopher looked so appeal-
ing, so helpless, and, at the same time, so jolly. And who
knows, perhaps he had hit upon something original and profound. One of the greatest of philosophers had been Democ-
ritus, known as the Laughing Philosopher. I promised to
read the manuscript, at least in part. I did, in part. It had
all the spontaneity of the non-professional; that was clear.
It was full of goodwill and bad grammar and large words
often misused and sometimes invented (though the same
might be said of many technical and accredited philosophical

systems). There were the manhandling of major half-truths
and a disordered rag-tag and bobtail of conventional ideas
drawn from all over the map and from the whole history of
thought. It tried to combine the efficiency of Babbitt with
the detachment of Buddha, the goodwill of Christian love
and the hatred of religion, of Lucretius and Robert Ingersoll.
There was a great parade of first principles that harked back
to Herbert Spencer, though Mr. R—— had apparently only
just heard of the latter. But the first principles contradicted
each other and often were not intelligible at all. The vast
opus could not by any stretch of the imagination be called a
contribution to knowledge or to thought, however much it
was an expression of sincerity and goodwill to mankind. The
jolly little man seemed greatly distressed a week or so later
when he appeared again and I tried, gently, to tell him some
of these impressions of mine. He took his manuscript. He
thanked me. He said he knew I had tried hard to be sympathetic. But he had not expected the academic mind really to
understand what he was driving at. He seemed very sad.

I recall one other instance of a retired business-man-
philosopher with whom I had a more indirect acquaintance.
He did not ask me to read his Philosophy. In fact, a good
part of it was not yet written, though it was, he said, all
thought out in his head. He wished to know whether I knew
a young graduate student, competent in both writing and
philosophy, who could help him straighten out his thoughts
and help him put them into words. He offered a very generous payment. I found a competent young man who said he
would be grateful for the job. I warned him it might be a
bore and would certainly be a chore. It did turn out to be

an ennui though a profitable one. For a year at ten dollars a morning the young man spent each morning with the amateur philosopher. The "Philosophy," he assured me, was half mad, half banal. It was shot through none the less with gleams of common sense that the philosopher had acquired in forty years as a building contractor. Meanwhile, the graduate student was teaching his patron something of Plato and Aristotle and Kant. The youth suffered, for he had an aseptic sense of logical rigour, a bitter distaste for all loose largeness in philosophy, and the young intellectual's contempt for banality. But by the end of the year he had come to like his employer and, save that he had a dissertation to finish himself, would have accepted his philosopher's offer to continue their collaboration on a trip around the world together, taking the Philosophy with them.

Philosophy, too, with its large and noble sound, attracts on its periphery the sentimental and the mad. I still shudder a little thinking of the middle-aged woman, dressed in brilliant green, who one day turned her gleaming eyes on me in my office, into which, quite unknown to me, she had entered.

"What are the avenues to knowledge?" she asked, without further preamble.

"They are generally said to be sense or reason," I replied, categorically.

"You have left out the most important one," she said, leaning forward and pointing an accusing finger at me.

"You mean, perhaps, mysticism," I said, with a divination that was not very difficult.

"Yes," she said, "professional philosophers are always leaving that out. Now, there is a path to reality; it is founded on deep breathing and serenity. It . . ." Her voice had grown shrill, her eyes more gleaming. I became alarmed. I hastened to say I had a class that very moment.

I never saw her again, nor did I see again the beautifully gowned creature who was impresario of a series of philosophical lectures in one of the grand hotels, and promised me that philosophy could easily become a fashion, and if it won over the world of fashion, as did Christianity in Rome, it would conquer the world. I have often thought she had a point.

What surprises the amateur usually is the discovery that the things that seem to him so fresh, so new, so original, have already been canvassed many times in the history of thought. He is usually surprised that he is not the first to have doubted the Existence of the Self, to have thought of the Soul of the World, to have enunciated the idea of the Kingdom of God or the Brotherhood of Man. In the midst of second-rateness and triviality there is usually a grain of insight, usually an old insight, and there is something touching about the attempt of a man long lost in practical details to find or enunciate a system that will express the whole meaning of life and existence. These five-hundred-page systems may be absurd, but they are touching tributes to the sentiment of rationality, and I rather have sympathized with the Babbitt who has a secret longing to be Plato or Kant.

Once I was particularly touched. In a town in Colorado where I had been lecturing on æsthetics to a public forum, there sat a serious, sad, heavy, middle-aged man, who at the question period suddenly read aloud a definition of art that he had obviously not just invented. At the next forum he asked me whether I would have dinner with him. I did so. He had for two years been a tuberculosis patient, living in a dreary boarding-house. After dinner he took me to his sad little room. He had been a singer in New York; he had never thought much about life, had been too busy. But here in the forced leisure of tuberculosis he had begun to think, and he opened a table drawer—here was a philosophy of life. It looked about the usual five hundred pages. It was, I feared, the worst, and my fears were realized. But you could not be too hard upon a man trying to think about the meaning of life in the shadow of death. On the other hand, the mere possibility of dying had not made him a philosopher. Nor does practical experience prevent business men, or even dictators or famous doctors, from sentimentalism or ineptitude when they try, late in life, to think in an orderly system about final matters.

One grows a little impatient (life in a university is, as William James pointed out, a series of interruptions anyway). But one ought not to be too quick. One of these days an obscure amateur will walk in with a system that, cutting through the professional vocabularies, the obfuscation of academic issues, will plumb to the very subsoil of reality. And we professionals will not recognize it. Perhaps we have often evinced such failures of insight.

I do not think I have failed to recognize the philosophical temper, though, where I have seen it outside the academy. It turns up in unexpected quarters. I had come to the radio shop in Bennington, Vermont, because on the hillside where I was living for the summer my battery radio would not work. The kindly, middle-aged, spinsterish-looking woman in the shop assured me all it needed was new batteries.

"Where do you live in the winter?" she asked.

"New York," I replied.

"And what do you do?"

"I teach."

"And what do you teach?"

"Philosophy."

"Philosophy!" she said, jumping up. "Why, we're philosophers here ourselves, especially my brother. . . . John!" she called. A quiet-looking, bespectacled, grey-haired man appeared from behind a door. "John, this gentleman is a philosopher.

"My brother is a philosopher too, a true philosopher," she said, turning to me, "only he puts his philosophy in verse. John, have you any of those poems in your desk?"

He blushed and said that they were at home.

"What," said the sister, looking at me, "is your philosophy?" and she sat down prepared to have the answer at once.

"Oh," I said, "I tell that to people all year. I like to use the vacations to find out other people's. What is yours?"

"Living in accordance with Nature," she said, "and seeing things as they are, and knowing that if you do, you are on the road to happiness. My brother put it in a poem once, and I write poems myself."

"A very great poet once said something like that in a poem," I remarked sententiously. "Lucretius."

"Well, I don't know about Lucretius," said the sister, "but we've thought that for ourselves, haven't we, John? Where do you live? Perhaps we could drive over some time and tell you about it . . . and talk over each other's philosophy. Philosophy is something to talk about, isn't it?"

"Nothing better," I said. "Plato said it was the only way to learn it."

A week later toward sunset the brother and sister philosophers turned up on my hilltop. They had brought the poems, too. For twenty years in their home after hours at their electrical shop, and apparently during it, in the quiet of a Vermont town they had made their peace with Nature. They had passed from childhood church-going to adolescent scepticism, to a contented sense of the world of Nature in which they were living, and of the good and evils which were part of its course. The brother read me an Emersonian soliloquy and the sister a Wordsworthian lyric. Neither of them had read Emerson or Wordsworth. But they had the former's sense of something far more deeply interfused, the latter's awareness of a movement in things entitled to be called divine, and a sober joy in it. And as they talked I realized more than I usually do what it means to say that poets speak the intuitions of the race, and say for mankind what it could not say itself. Neither the brother nor the sister wrote like Emerson or Wordsworth, but quite on their own they had come the same path. A non-functioning digestion had brought me into the presence of a philosopher in a French provincial town; a non-functioning radio had introduced me to two in Bennington, and oddly enough, it was not at the college there either.

My Vermont friends were aware that they had a "philosophy." I am not sure that Mathilde is aware of it, though she has for twenty years now run the elevator in Philosophy Hall. She has seen generations of students pass by; she has transported to and from their offices professors of philosophy, English literature, Romance languages, Sanskrit, Persian, Arabic, and Slavonic. She is invariably cheerful, though she is not always well. Her cheerfulness is aided, perhaps, by the

calendar she has in her car, containing, along with the days
and the seasons, appropriate and helpful cheering sentiments.
Mathilde has, perhaps, never read T. H. Green's famous
essay called "My Station and Its Duties," but in her car she
has found her station and has for twenty years now, to students and professors alike, communicated a wonderful sense
of friendly, maternal interest and of philosophical detachment and calm. I am not sure she takes too seriously the
books we write, the courses we give, or the courses students
take; but I know that many of us take seriously the serene,
unillusioned kindliness and friendliness with which she has
learned in her car to survey the world. "I have seen people
go up and up," she once remarked; "I continue to go up and
down." And while doing so, she has found and communicated wisdom and peace.

So, too, has Maria, who conducts with devoted efficiency
and pride of art, my small ménage at home. Maria is a good
Catholic, though she does not take her religion too solemnly;
she respects learning, though she reads nothing but what she
calls the "tragedy" papers. She has no interest save her job,
the Church, and her family, about whom, for ten years now,
I have heard and which, I take it on the faith of her absolute
honesty, exists. The order of the seasons and the calendar of
the saints and the pattern of the domestic season have given
her a quiet content and a shrewd estimate of the various people, full, as she puts it, of college words, who come to visit
me. Quiet content and shrewd estimates of people and things
and acceptance of a narrow round of life do not, perhaps,
constitute a philosophy. But they are something, perhaps,
favourably to be compared with it. Maria's is a simple wisdom. But the upshot of most wisdoms is simple, and Maria

has achieved a kind of order in her life that few people, full of college words, have been able to achieve in megalopolitan New York. Maria left on my table once a little manual issued by her Church to parishioners. It is an explanation of the Mass, and it is called the Key to the Kingdom of Heaven. Maria has found the key at least to serenity. Without college words either.

"I prayed for your health this morning," she said one day on returning from Mass.

"Do you think it will help?" I asked.

"It will if you believe it," she said, simply. Many philosophers have found more complicated ways of expounding the nature and value of belief.

A simple serenity is not a philosophy. But quite outside the technical circles men have arrived at what may more properly be called such. I rather wish certain men of affairs I know had set down their philosophies. The Boston surgeon, for instance, who, having been so much involved in crises of life and death, had arrived at a general sense of what life held and what its limits were. He is dead himself now, but I wish before he had died he had written down what he had come to believe. It might have been academically "amateur," but it would have been serious; it would have been reflections that arose from life actually encountered, rather than merely books remembered, though of books, especially those of the Greeks, he had read many, and he had seen experience with the classical directness.

I rather wish the judge I know, whose sharp, quick mind is incorrigibly speculative as well as practical, would write his ultimate reflections. Perhaps his metaphysics would be sketchy, but he could write, I am sure, a "Treatise on Human Nature" that would compare not unfavourably with David Hume's. For one thing, he has some of that great Scot's canniness, and from a long concern with the law, he would make distinctions only when they made a difference. It seems a pity that the late Justice Cardozo, who could talk with such poetic and precise wisdom on so many themes, wider even than his wide conception of the law, has not left behind his reflections on what were so much his preoccupations, the spiritual dilemmas of the modern man. It seems to me rather a pity that so many men who have known the world, and been prompted to reflect upon its meaning, should not have tried to put that meaning down. Doctors and lawyers and statesmen have taken to writing their autobiographies. I wish it would become a mode for them to write their views of Nature, or their conceptions of life. The best of them, I am sure, would be contributions to philosophy; their wisdom might be a little too much of this world, but it would be wisdom, and, at the very least, it would be interesting to know what our conquerors thought of the meaning of the world they had conquered. But if such books should be written, I would wish that they be written honestly out of reflection upon lives actually lived and encountered. The philosophers without portfolio might well leave it to the professional philosophers to write their philosophies out of other people's books.

FOURTEEN

Little Older New York

EVERY philosophy is expressed by a philosopher and, though all philosophers inhabit the same earth and live under the same sky, the local nook in which each grew up inevitably affects the cadence and the contour of his thought. Plato said the philosopher was the spectator of all time and all existence, but he himself never forgot the palæstra and the market-places of Athens. He makes Socrates say he could never be long distant from Athens, and that he would rather die there than live in exile. Kant thundered apodictic certainties, but there are pietistic traces of provincial Königsberg that tincture his cosmos. There is Parisian elegance in Bergson's pages, and rural Vermont lives in the passion for democracy of John Dewey's social thought. As a humble worker in the same spiritual vineyard I may be pardoned for not outgrowing my own corner of the universe. For despite any ambition to see things, Spinoza-like, under the form of eternity, I am reminded always of the forms of living which will seem to me most intimate simply because I grew up in a certain section of Manhattan in the first decade of the twen-

tieth century. Any vision of timeless things I shall ever have
will inevitably be coloured by a childhood spent in a little
older New York.

Everyone, I suppose, who has had even a relatively happy
childhood, grows nostalgic about it. Doubtless, Johnny, the
fourteen-year-old son of my college classmate, J—— M——,
will look back thirty years from now on the days when one
put up with old-fashioned, sightless radio, when hardly anyone owned a private aeroplane, when most apartments did
not have air-conditioning, when manners were easy and in-
formal, when children did what they pleased and spelled as
they pleased in progressive schools, and there was exciting
news in the papers about China and Spain. But, seen through
a sentimental haze or not, the New York of thirty to forty
years ago seems to me now a very much simpler and more
liveable and lovable place than the one the New Yorker lives
in today. Older people confirm me in the remembered impressions of a child. I recall a simpler and more friendly Manhattan: the Manhattan of bicycling even in the centre of
town, of seeing with disdainful amusement the first horseless
carriages, of sitting in the open-air German beer gardens with
their hedges of potted plants (the word German in those days
had a genial sound), of boarding the open trolley cars which
marked, more than flowers, the advent of spring, and of
chatting with the friendly neighbours across the hall. There
was no radio; there was only the ancient horned phonograph;
but there was Schumann heard on the neighbour's piano or
by one's sister on that of one's own family. There was no
subway, but there were, to a boy, delightful rides on the
elevated when one sat opposite the motorman's box watching his casual expertness with the controller and the airbrake,

and the neat way he slowed for the curve at Fifty-Third Street, or coasted from Ninety-Third to Eighty-First. One had heard tales of the dead man's handle; the way the train would come to a halt if the motorman should suddenly die and his hand fall from the control. I used to watch in the morbid hope that that might happen sometime before my very eyes as I watched the motorman through the transparent glass window of his little cabin.

My family lived most of the time I went to school and high school on Morningside Avenue, just below Morningside Park. It was a quiet, bourgeois neighbourhood, though neither I nor anybody else knew the word much then. Harlem meant not the world of Negroes or of "swing" but of middle-class domesticity. Indeed, some of the pleasantest streets in the city were, and are, those up in the One Hundred and Thirties, one of them still with beautiful shade trees. Morningside Avenue was extremely quiet; there were no autos, though by the time I was fifteen one began to see a few. Harlem had a life of its own, a kind of village duplicate of downtown. There was "Koch's," the highly respectable department store on One Hundred and Twenty-Fifth Street. There was the West End Theatre on One Hundred and Twenty-Fifth Street just off Morningside Avenue, where the New York hits used to come late in the season or the next season for a week's stand. As a child you were taken (by the time you were fourteen or fifteen, you went alone or with a friend) on Saturday afternoon to see, a season late, *The Girl of the Golden West,* David Warfield in *The Return of Peter Grimm,* or *The Wizard of Oz.* A little further east, just off Eighth Avenue, was the Penny Arcade, where you could have a view of Palestine or the Wild West for a penny, a brief moving picture; or try your strength with weights; or get weighed; or have your fortune told; or hear sung by various sopranos the ballads of the day: "In the Shade of the Old Apple Tree," "Down by the Old Mill Stream," and that rousing song from *Floradora*—"Tararara Boom-di-ay." Still further east, around the corner on Seventh Avenue, was the Alhambra Theatre, one of the once nation-wide chain of Keith vaudeville theatres, also filled with children of the neighbourhood on Saturday afternoons. It was a changeless routine. First the acrobat, then a comedy turn, then a song and dance team, then a monologist, working up to some comedy star such as Eva Tanguay with her mad reckless song, "I Don't Care," or some famous "legitimate" actress appearing at a climactic moment, just before intermission, in one of her famous scenes or in a one-act play. I am not sure Ethel Barrymore came to the Alhambra—at least in my time—but I think she did. And I believe her "vehicle" was Barrie's *The Twelve-Pound Look,* with her famous line: "That's all there is; there isn't any more," delivered in her deep, dignified contralto that half hid a wise laughter.

Still further east, 'way across town, near Lexington Avenue, was the Harlem Opera House, which, when I knew it, had a stock company that every week played a different play for twelve performances, two each day. I must have seen two dozen plays or so there, but the only two I remember are *The Old Homestead* and *Sherlock Holmes*. Each in its way was typical of the repertoire and the acting, which I thought superb. It was not, I suppose, but greater acting has seldom since produced in me so complete and wonderfully compelling an illusion.

And it was a great treat afterwards to go into Childs—the

original neolithic Childs, with white-topped tables—and to eat, as I wish I were still competent to do today, griddle cakes.

But life to a boy in Harlem in the nineteen-tens was not all Saturday afternoon theatres and griddle cakes. Even apart from school there were other amusements. The streetcars— at least to some of us—played the same role of adventure and speed that an auto might have for youngsters of today, possibly more. You went alone or with your family all the way up Amsterdam Avenue on a Saturday afternoon in spring, when the theatre season was over, to Fort George, where there was a miniature Coney Island. The ride was almost as much fun as the Ferris wheels, the merry-go-rounds, the popcorn at the end of it, especially as in the open trolleys with their cross seats you could sit up in front by the motorman and watch him clang his footbell, as the car blazed along at what seemed terrific speed once it got into the region of open lots, and woodland even, and farmland beyond One Hundred and Forty-Fifth Street. For a more ambitious trip there was, of course, Coney Island. That you were not allowed—at least till you were fifteen or sixteen—to do alone. In the first place it was a long and arduous trip. One had to start early, for there was the lengthy and interesting journey down to Brooklyn Bridge. Since the trip was part of the fun and time was not of the essence, one might even go by trolley instead of by elevated down to Brooklyn Bridge. The best way of going was to take the horse car, the Dinkey Car we called it—one of the few remaining ones in the city—down St. Nicholas Avenue across to One Hundred and Tenth Street and Madison Avenue; then on the Madison Avenue trolley, a matter of about fifty-five minutes, to Brooklyn Bridge. It was exciting to watch the changes in neighbourhoods and topography, and to admire the way the car took the stiff grade up past the armoury at Ninety-Fifth Street, to pass through the brownstone elegance, even then, of the Seventies and Sixties, past our doctor's house, into the busy Forties, through the shops and crush and trucking—the car began to move very slowly, and there was considerable clanging—and finally, under the elevated on the Bowery—still a name to conjure with as a legend—with its toughs and foreigners and saloons. Finally one arrived at Brooklyn Bridge with its trolleys marked with many strange Brooklyn destinations, to take another open-air trolley, through miles of country-looking streets, to Coney Island itself. I seem to remember the trip more than the destination. One had, I recall, a shore dinner at Feltman's and did all the concessions at Luna Park and Dreamland before one of them—I forget which—was burnt down. One had the thrill and the discomfort of the scenic railway, and at dusk one had the long ride back to Brooklyn Bridge. By that time one sleepily assented to going home on the speedier "L."

But it was not necessary to go so far afield for diversion. Right close by, in Morningside Park, there was coasting in winter, with the added adventure of being possibly interfered with by the "toughs" who lived in the slummy block between Manhattan and Eighth Avenues, a block east of the Park. There was "dry" coasting even in spring, when one was very young. I, for instance, had an Irish Mail, a child's bright red handcar. A chum used to help me transport it to the top of the park, and as a reward was allowed to speed with me down the hill that ran around the Park, sitting backwards, and using his shoes as a brake. That occupation was finally ended by a policeman who told us we were an obstruction to traffic. There wasn't much traffic to be obstructed. Most of the land at the top of the park was still rocks that is all apartment houses now, and Philosophy Hall, where my office has been for the past twenty years, had not yet been built. Once on one of our rides we were engaged in conversation by a Columbia freshman; we could tell he was a freshman by his small black cap with its white button. We reported for days around the block that we had actually talked with a bona fide Columbia student, but nobody believed us.

There was roller skating, and "cops and robbers," and ball games as well, though my near-sightedness prevented me from participating in the latter. There were indoor games, particularly "Parcheesi," in which one did not need to be an athlete; and there was "collecting." Country boys may collect various interesting things, birds' nests and what not, but I am sure they could not have had more fun than we had collecting streetcar transfers and time-tables. I don't know who started it in our neighbourhood, but I know quite a ritual and set of standards developed. The streetcar lines along the avenues in New York issued red and green transfers: red for south bound, green for north. The crosstown lines issued white ones. By what logic I know not, the red transfers counted ten dollars, the green two dollars, and the crosstown five. The crosstown ones, as a matter of fact, should, by those laws of supply and demand about which I learned myself when I in time became a Columbia student, have counted higher, for it seldom happened that one's friends or relatives took only a crosstown trip without using their transfers. Suburban transfers counted twenty-five, and those of distant cities, like Philadelphia and Boston, one hundred. It was, of course, chiefly through friends and relatives that we acquired transfers. We became a perfect plague to the adults in the neighbourhood. Transfers became for us a kind of currency, and one of the chief things for which we used them was railroad time-tables, which also had relatively established values. The great trunk lines of the East, the Pennsylvania and the New York Central and the B. and O.,were worth about a hundred dollars each. Those West and South anywhere up to five hundred, for being further away they were harder to come by. Those of us whose parents travelled much for business or pleasure were in luck. I myself developed into quite a capitalist for a while, for I dragooned my father once into bringing me home from the West the time-tables of the Santa Fe, the Great Northern, the Nickel Plate, the Canadian Pacific. For the last, on the ground that it was from a foreign country, I received a thousand dollars.

One of our group discovered one day by accident something that quite disrupted our financial system and produced a period of inflation for a time while we all aped his discovery. He found that in the offices of some of the New York railroads there were racks containing the time-tables of almost all the railroads in the country. It became quite a game for us to visit the offices and quietly, though tremblingly, denude the racks. If we had any doubts as to whether it was stealing or not, an angry clerk one day made it clear what the railroads thought about it, and time-tables from remote railroads went back to their usual prices.

Our crowd consisted of the boys who lived on Morningside Avenue or on the "nice" blocks of brownstone houses just off it. We were all the sons of middle-class families, and our respectable fathers, many of them, wore top hats on

Sunday, a formality which somehow seemed to consort with that simple epoch, like the stiff collars even we small boys wore, and which did not seem to us at all odd.

But just one block east lay another world. There was a row of tenements which poured forth upon the street after school hours the One Hundred and Twentieth Street Gang. They seemed very tough indeed to me, and we all, particularly myself, with our stiff collars and blue suits, seemed mollycoddles to them. I passed through that street afternoons sometimes on my way to the Deutsche Apotheke of Kohler and Wohl. On certain days—Hallowe'en, for instance—it required real physical courage. I knew some of those boys by sight and some to speak to from seeing them at Public School 10. But, without knowing much about Middletown, without having read proletarian novels, I still felt—we all felt—a chasm between us. The sturdier among us on Morningside Avenue rather emulated the toughs' ways and pretended to their sophistication. But I was not one of the sturdier ones, and their voices, their words, and their fists frightened me. I also in some vague way felt sorry for them, especially on hot June evenings when I knew almost all of our crowd would soon be off in the country. But I also had a great moral revulsion: they used bad words, they shouted at each other, they pommelled each other in a way that, in the code on Morningside Avenue, was not considered very nice. Passing to and from Kohler and Wohl's, I could often overhear what they thought of me. Once or twice they looked threatening, but on the whole one came through unscathed, without more than the insults of "Four Eyes" for one's spectacles and "Mamma's Boy" for one's blue suit and

"Whitey"—not without good humour—for one's blond hair.

My world and my standards and those of the Hundred and Twentieth Street Gang came to a crucial conflict once. I was on my way from Kohler and Wohl's with some headache powders for my mother. It was growing dark, about five o'clock one crisp October afternoon. The Gang was out in full force. I tried to walk as invisibly as possible. A ragamuffin about my own age suddenly seized me by the shoulder. "Gimme all you got," he said. I was at once frightened and outraged, but fright conquered. I meekly gave him my fountain pen, the new Waterman I had received for my birthday, a batch of transfers amounting to over a thousand dollars, my watch. He tore up the transfers.

"Got any money?" he said.

"Twenty-five cents. What," I said and with some singular surge of moral scruple, "what do you want to do with it?"

"Cigarettes," he said.

Now in our neighbourhood and among my friends a cigarette at that period, even for adults, seemed the last word in moral disintegration. Some reformist zeal overcame my cowardice. "I'll give you the quarter I've got if you'll promise not to spend it on cigarettes," I said.

The tough looked at me strangely. Something in the request puzzled him.

"What's the idea?" he asked in astonishment.

"They're coffin nails," I said; "they're bad for you, and you'll die early. You really oughtn't to smoke, you know."

He eyed me with wonder and compassion.

"Say, you're a good guy," he said, and to my own intense

astonishment he restored my watch and my fountain pen, and held out his hand for the quarter I had in my fingers.

"Come and have some pop with me," he said.

Before I could stop the words from coming out of my mouth, I said: "I must bring this package home to my mother."

He looked at me with more wonder and a tinge of contempt. But whenever the toughs beleaguered me thereafter, and he was about, he'd say: "Say, let that guy alone; he's all right."

It's the only moral conquest I can remember making.

For the most part our world on Morningside Avenue and the streets immediately adjacent was a closed and tranquil one. There were a few class distinctions: two of the group went to the Horace Mann School, which seemed to the families of the rest of us a little pretentious. One of us moved away to one of the early elevator apartments over by the river and he warned us to dress up properly when we came to see him. We leagued together not to, and never did. Summer evenings we would sit on the railings of the park, singing the current songs, occasionally go to nickelodeons, the movies in stores, which had just come in, and on summer afternoons ride out on our bicycles to Van Cortlandt Park or the still verdant West Bronx.

The subway opened, the apartment house era began; we grew older. One of us died of appendicitis at sixteen; it seemed like the collapse of a world. Several moved away. The Park Commissioner, I notice, has streamlined Morningside Park. There are bright new railings; the park has been landscaped, the big rock half-way up, from which we used to begin coasting, has been smoothed down. Most of the buildings on Morningside Avenue seem to have been turned into rooming-houses; the whole quarter seems desolate. Kohler and Wohl's, I noticed the other day, has become a chain store, with a lunch counter. The Dinkey Car is no more. And S——, who was the Prince Charming of Morningside Avenue, who used to recite so elegantly on Sunday evenings and was the Beau Brummel of the Morningside crowd, now lives on Park Avenue, and, being a movie magnate, spends most of his time on Broadway. We meet at theatres occasionally, and invariably remind each other nostalgically of a little older New York. Johnny and his friends will doubtless do that forty years from now, reminding each other of the black-and-white movies, the one-man buses, the cumbersome old disk records, and the motor-cars with the motors in front.

I learned to know worlds elsewhere, and certainly the university world I now live in (now, as it was then, just across the park) is a very different one. My realm of values is no longer measured by streetcar transfers; the little older New York is gone, and I think of it seldom. But I suspect that tiny neighbourhood will linger subterraneously in any thinking, however cosmic in its theme, on which I might ambitiously embark.

FIFTEEN

Syrian Sophomores

AFTER a certain number of years of teaching one awaits no surprises or perhaps becomes incapacitated for having any. The academic pattern has become familiar, and one is prepared to believe that in this educational place, at this academic time, things will always be about the same. One cherishes, however, the illusion that the pattern is not the same everywhere, that if, for example, one were lecturing in Timbuktu, or conducting a seminar in Somaliland, students would be different and perhaps one would think of new things to say, or even think of new things.

Such reflections recall the story of an actress who, having played with moderate success in New York, confessed her ambitions to a companion on shipboard. She wished to repeat her triumphs on the stage in France in French, in Italy in Italian, in Germany in German. "Now," said her unfeeling companion, "you have only to learn to act in English in New York."

Academic persons, too, have their exotic hungers. The *mise-en-scène* has become too routine; the freshmen are all identical, the sophomores are more drearily because less freshly so; the faces and the food at the Faculty Club have become a dull habit; the academic calendar is depressingly unvarying. The feeling grows that it is not the academic life that has become stale, but its local setting. Even visits for a week or a term to neighbouring institutions are not enough. The small college, it is true, is not the large university; it has its different, intimate charm. The country college is not the city one, patently and often delightfully enough. There are in autumn no reddening maples on a city block. It is only a stone's throw from Columbia to Amherst or Williams or Wesleyan; it might be several thousand miles. Overnight one is among the colonnades and the Virginia gentlemen of Charlottesville, or the homespun and pastoral kindness and trans-Allegheny common-sense of Wabash College, Indiana. I had known these things were true, and I had enjoyed discovering them. And yet things never were different enough. I had always envied the half-missionary professors in China and Japan. They came back trailing clouds of Oriental glory, though their clothes and accents, and even their points of view, had not changed. I had pictured Lafcadio Hearn's delights in lecturing on English poetry to Japanese students, to the tinkling, I liked to imagine, of neighbouring temple bells. I had friends, indeed, who had taught in the Orient and who seemed and claimed to have learned as much from their students as they had taught them, to have borrowed as much from Oriental pupils and from the novel setting as they had brought to them. Sometimes, it is true, I had had that same experience on my own campus, but after ten years or more at the same institution, I felt I had become anæsthetized, at least for the time being, to all that local students could teach me, or to such atmosphere as one could breathe in on Morningside Heights. It was, therefore, with no small pleasure one day in Rome about seven years ago, that, being on leave of absence from Columbia, I received an invitation from the American University at Beirut in Syria to give three lectures there on the Philosophy of Religion. I was, somebody there had learned, on my way to Syria. I was planning to follow as well as I could the footsteps of St. Paul, about whom, in possibly a ten thousandth book on the theme, I was planning to say something new. In Syria was Damascus, and from Syria one went to Antioch. It turned out, however, that I learned most in Syria not from the Street Called Straight in Damascus, where they show you the alleged spot where Paul was lowered in a basket. I learned nothing at Antioch, for I did not reach there. Unlike Paul, I was given pause by the difficulties of transport, far less arduous, I am prepared to admit, than they were in his day. What I learned was little about Paul, and what I did learn I found out from Syrian sophomores, from whom I found out or had confirmed something about the nature of all sophomores and about American education and perhaps ultimately about education itself.

The American University at Beirut, as everyone knows (at least everyone in Beirut and in Presbyterian circles in America) was founded about sixty years ago as a mission college. It was intended, by means of a four-year American college course, with attendant chapel services, to bring Christianity to the heathen of the Near East. Its missionary work has long since become subtler and no less difficult or rewarding; it has tried for many years now to do just what colleges in America try to do: to bring education to students.

Syria is under French mandate now, of course, but A.U.B. English, as it is called locally (and it is very good English, too), is encountered in remote spots all over Syria. I found it to be the chief means of communication in the bazaars of Damascus.

The American University at Beirut is really a typical small-town American college. Its organization and its atmosphere, especially its faculty social life, are simply Connecticut or New Hampshire transplanted to the Mediterranean. Its site is certainly different, perched as it is on a headland over a ravishing Mediterranean bay with sometimes snow-capped mountains visible from the campus, and always the intensely blue sea. In setting it is a semi-Oriental Riviera. But in the President's house, and among the senior faculty members and among the staff (the young men directly out of college who come out for three years), I felt I had been here before. The older faculty members, some of whom had been teaching in Syria for thirty years and spoke Arabic fluently, had none the less succeeded in creating the atmosphere and the expectations, social and moral, of a small sectarian college town. The *Atlantic Monthly* was on the living-room table, and all that was missing was Colonial architecture.

The students were another matter. They suggested not Middletown but Tarsus, said to have been the crossroads of the ancient world. There were coal-black youths from the Sudan, Jewish as well as Arab students from Palestine, Coptic Christians and Mohammedans from all over Syria, and a Persian prince, and (I could scarcely believe my ears, but the accent was unmistakable) some Brooklyn boys studying in the excellent medical school.

It was a frightening challenge to speak about the Philosophy of Religion to a student body of that mixed provenance. But I had just heard Gene Tunney, on a world tour, address a chapel audience at Beirut. He had spoken, apparently quite intelligibly to his audience, on themes redolent of an American Boy Scout morality. And surely there was no better or more appropriate place to speak on the themes of comparative religion than here where Coptic Christians, Mohammedans, Jews, and Presbyterians were mingled in the matrix of an American college curriculum, studying English by the sea on whose shores all the religions of the ancient world had grown and flourished. Was I not engaged in studying the diverse origins of Christianity in the maelstrom of the Mediterranean cults of the first century? The maelstrom was still perpetuated here. The thought gave me courage and so too did the elaborate yet spontaneous courtesy of the students with whom I had spoken. Two of them took the odd trouble of teaching me by rote enough Arabic to make a few introductory remarks in that language. They said it would be a compliment to the audience and the audience would feel more at home with me. I followed their suggestion, apologizing for not continuing in Arabic as there might be a few present who did not understand. Either that introduction or something else seemed to put me *en rapport* with my listeners; after the first five minutes it seemed as natural to be talking about philosophy in West Hall on the Beirut campus as in Philosophy Hall at Columbia. I felt I was among friends.

That feeling was pleasantly and, as it turned out, oddly confirmed the next day. I was sitting in my room in the guest dormitory, staring out at the sea in incubative intervals—or I liked to think they were such—in my preparations for the second lecture. There was a knock on the door. I opened to see a pleasant young man, squat, black-haired, dark-skinned. I tried at once to guess his nationality. Syrian, I judged. I tried to guess his year in the college. Sophomore, somehow, I was sure.

He was elaborately apologetic about disturbing me. But he had some questions to ask. I motioned him to a chair.

"Do you ever give personal advice to students?" he asked.

"When I am asked, I cannot always refrain," I replied.

"Well, I've come for personal advice," he said. "I was at your lecture last night, and I felt you could give it to me."

"But there was nothing personal about the lecture," I said. "It was pretty remote from any personal problems whatever, as I remember it."

"Yes, but still I have a feeling that you would understand student problems, and I've got some."

"You are very flattering," I said, "but I should feel very hesitant about giving advice here. I hesitate at home, but I suspect the problems of a Syrian sophomore—you are a sophomore, aren't you?"—he nodded—"are rather different from those of a sophomore in America. I've only been at the University of Beirut three days, and in Syria less than a week, and I've never been to the Near East before."

He fumbled nervously. "Just the same," he said, "there are a few things I should like to ask you."

"Let me ask you one thing first myself," I said. "Are you Syrian?"

"No," he said, "Egyptian, Mohammedan; my father is a

business man in Cairo. We don't get on awfully well any more. Especially since I've come away to college. I've grown rather irreligious, you know, and it makes trouble when I come home."

"You've possibly turned Christian," I said.

"Oh, no," he said, looking shocked, "nothing like that. I just have lost my religion altogether, and a sense of family."

"And you don't want to go into business, do you?"

He looked surprised at the guess, but went on.

"Do young men of eighteen or nineteen in the West begin to have very different ideas from those of their parents?" he asked.

I smiled. "This sounds just like home."

"You can't tell how upsetting it is, all these new ideas one gets at college," he said, "about freedom and dancing and sex and what not. I don't suppose Western students have to make so much of an adjustment; they don't come from one world to another when they come from home to college, do they? It's all one, the Western world, isn't it?"

My mind leaped back to "Tex" Goldschmidt, who had come to Columbia from a strict Lutheran family in San Antonio, Texas; to Stanley Smith, who had arrived in New York from a strict and genteel suburban family in Verona, New Jersey; to Joe Farrell, who had been brought up in a Catholic parochial school in Boston; to Arthur Calder, the son of a pious Scotch widow; to the young Puritan from a New Hampshire village who had come not only to New York but also to Gide and to Henry James. I told my young Egyptian about them and how they, too, in college had come upon a new world in which each, in his own way, had had to make some adjustment. He looked intensely surprised.

"But fathers don't expect their sons in the West to follow the same way of life that they led, do they?" he said.

"Many of them do."

"And to have the same ideas?" he said dubiously.

"Even that," I said.

"And do the ideas students in the West get at college seem to them so different from what they hear at home, as many of the ideas I've picked up in classes here and from other students appear to me?"

"Quite as much," I insisted.

"But the changes in life cannot be so rapid in the West as they have been here in the last twenty-five years."

"Oh, yes, they can, I am sure; but I rather thought," I said, "that here in the East things don't change so rapidly."

He looked at me again in the greatest surprise.

"I went to the Muslim University in Cairo," I explained, "where students seem to be listening as they did in the Middle Ages, and, I am told, to the same things, the Koran chiefly, and explanations of it."

"Oh, but that's rather a backwater; none of *my* friends go there. I'm talking about *modern* youth in the East."

"Well, what personal advice does a modern youth in the Near East want?" I said.

"I wondered what I ought to do about ideas," he replied, "and *should* I go into my father's business when I get my degree. My father expects me to be a business man, but I don't want to, and all the professions are overcrowded. It's very difficult for a young man these days, especially a college man here in the Near East. What do *you* advise me to do?"

I have in my time advised young men not to go into the teaching profession, not to become professional philosophers, especially if they were genuinely philosophers; I have with a certain glibness told them they were born lawyers or business men or journalists or writers, but I hesitated, I admit, to advise this young Egyptian as to a career. Though, as I thought about it afterwards, I reflected there was no special reason for diffidence. My Egyptian visitor was worried about a career in Cairo, Egypt, and had trouble accommodating his ideas to those of his father and his family there. But it might just as well have been Cairo, Illinois. A sophomore hailing from there would also have had a naïve faith that a professor could advise about a career and counsel about morals. I once had written about a youth named Richard Kane whom college had "unprepared for life." Here he was, slightly darker-skinned, on the shore of the Sophoclean sea. I had not in months felt so near home.

I felt at home, too, but less so, the next day when crossing the campus I ran into a group of young Syrians who hailed me and said they had some questions to ask. "We've been discussing the difference between moral standards in the East and West," one of them said.

"A profound question to raise on a Saturday in spring," I said.

"Well, we have, and there are one or two questions we should like to ask you," one of them said. He looked at his companions in some obvious embarrassment.

"Go ahead; ask him," one of the group insisted encouragingly.

"Well," the embarrassed young man said, "well, is it true that in the West young men actually go out dancing with young women without necessarily creating a scandal by doing it?"

"Oh, yes," I said, "quite the usual thing, really; it happens every day."

"But it would ruin a Mohammedan girl's reputation, and a young man's too, in some ways," he said. "We wondered whether that is really true, what we hear about the West, that young men and women associate quite freely. I doubt whether that will ever be true here in Syria."

"But you do go dancing," I said, "don't you?"

"Oh, yes," was the reply, "but not with respectable girls; that is, not with respectable *Mohammedan* girls. It's a different story with Jewish or Christian ones. The West must be a very different place."

We adjourned to a neighbouring café for some of the Arabic coffee, with its pure and clear flavour that I had come to love. We discussed the differences in collegiate morals of New York and of Syria, the differences seeming to disappear as we talked.

I had once forgathered with a similar group (who called themselves The Thinkers) in Urbana, Illinois. The only difference in temper I could feel (and it was not so much a difference in temper as a difference in form) was in the sense of form itself that these young men had. Centuries of tradition or ritual of courtesy seemed to be bred in them. American undergraduates would have been no less kindly and hospitable, but there would have been a less finished expression of their kindness and hospitality.

"The Syrians have a great gift for friendliness," I said as we finally rose to leave.

"They have that gift, sir, to those who have it," was the suave reply from one of the group. I have known only one sophomore who would have thought of that reply in

America, and he was regarded as fantastically precious by his classmates—and by me.

But I was to have one other introduction to the student mind of Syria, this time to a senior, not to a sophomore. I was again sitting in my room in West Hall. The visitor this time was a tall, coal-black youth with shining teeth and eyes. He was dressed in a neat, blue pin-striped suit, a handkerchief peeping out of his breast pocket and a book (it turned out to be a novel by Virginia Woolf) under his arm. His accent was not that of the American University at Beirut, but distinctly English. Except for that I should have been inclined to guess, had I met him on a train, that he was an educated American Negro.

I wondered whether he, too, was coming for advice. He was not. He began at once by saying that he had not any very good claim on my time, that he had no special problem, that he had not even come to discuss the subjects which I had touched on in the lectures. He wished only to talk over some things he had been reading lately. What did I think of Virginia Woolf? Did I not think Aldous Huxley carried his sceptical cynicism too far? Was T. S. Eliot really such a first-rate critic as people pretended? He rather doubted it, but he was a great poet, or at least technically a very competent one. He had heard he ought to read Gide and Proust but he did not read French and it was hard to come by them in English. It was hard to come by books at all where he lived. (The last time I had listened to this flood of literary undergraduate criticism, it was in New York, though in that accent I had most recently heard it in Oxford.)

"Where *do* you live?" I asked.

"In the middle of the Sudan," he said.

"Pretty far off from literary interests, isn't it?" I said. "Are you going back there?"

"Yes," he said a little sadly. "I've been sent here on a scholarship and I expect the Sudan is the place I shall go back to. I shall be a schoolmaster in a small village. I shan't have much chance to talk about this sort of thing." His eyes brightened. "But one could become a poet out there, I think. You have no conception of the distance and the solitude—it's made for meditation; and the bright clarity of the stars—have you ever been to the desert?"

"*Just,*" I replied.

"But you should live there to know what it's like. It's lonely and splendid. Only I shan't have any one to talk to, really, and a writer needs people."

"He doesn't need literary people, does he?" I asked. "You could write just the same."

"Yes, but one loses touch, and, what's more, one loses English."

"You could write in Arabic."

"There isn't a public for Arabic; those who read, read the Koran really: and I want to write in English."

I have often since thought of my lonely black schoolmaster in his village in the Sudan, though no lonelier, I think, than a poet I know in North Dakota, nor than a man of letters on the plains, almost as spacious as those of the Sudan, of Kansas. I had often suspected that there is no geography of the spirit, and a sojourn among students in Syria convinced me I had been right—or did it? I suddenly reflected that the pattern of American college life was surprisingly definite; this son of the Sudan had for four years been living, spiritually speaking, on American soil. And there are Americans, too, in the midst of their Sudans, lonely, amid distances and solitudes, and meditating, like this black youth, under the bright clarity of a starry Western sky, and far from any one who speaks their language or moves in their realm of spirit.

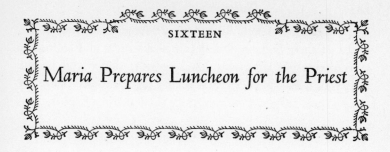

SIXTEEN

Maria Prepares Luncheon for the Priest

A STUDENT of philosophy likes to think of himself as rather magnificently homeless, his mind ranging freely in the great spaces between the stars,

Voyaging through strange seas of thought alone.

But a philosopher must live somewhere. I once heard a distinguished thinker say that the greatest philosophers in the nineteenth century all lived in hotels and that they were unmarried. Freedom from family obligations and the cares of a household might well be calculated to liberate the spirit for empyrean flights. But one must eat and sleep, have clean linen (unless like Diogenes one takes to a barrel). A philosopher must have a refuge, and in that respect I am very lucky.

Maria has been keeping house for me for nearly ten years. She has been in various parts of my family for more than twenty, and has known me since I was a college boy visiting my sister, at which time she would force milk upon me—"It'll keep up your strength; it'll keep you from falling in the gutter; it's just like food."

Maria came from Ireland at the age of eighteen, the seventh daughter of the second gardener on an Irish estate, as she told me for the first time the other day. She and her sister were sent to America by their mother. Somebody had said to the latter one day: "Mrs. Powers, why don't you send your daughters to America? There's gold on the streets there."

Maria and her sister came, and since then Maria has been in numerous households, as parlourmaid in a large brownstone house, nursemaid, cook. But since she has come to my apartment, she runs the whole establishment and (she says I am the first adult she has ever had to take care of) she takes very good care of me.

She is not very clear about what my work consists in, but she is convinced that it is very important, especially such of it as I do at home. She frequently tells people over the telephone that I must not be disturbed. "He is concentrating."

She has seen a good many professors at one time or another in the last ten years, and she is rather convinced that "brain work" destroys the nerves. But she found John Dewey, when he came one day in a snowstorm, a fine healthy old gentleman who looked very much like John Flynn, the old farmer in Galway, whom the children loved and feared.

Maria has been in New York over forty years, but her work, her church, and her sister—and occasionally trips downtown to do window-shopping—are all her connexion with it. Except what she reads in the "tragedy" papers, she reads nothing. I know a good deal about her church, for she brings me the parish magazine, tells me how long or how short the sermon was (she prefers the short ones), and I have an indirect connexion with it for I occasionally contribute to St.

Anthony's box for the poor via Maria. Maria is a very faithful Catholic. She never misses Mass, she observes most fast days, though the priest says working people need not do so; but she does not overdo religion, she tells me, like some people.

I know a good deal by hearsay about Maria's married, now widowed, sister. But I have to take her on faith in Maria's unimpeachable honesty, for that sister might be like Dickens's Mrs. Harris as far as my direct acquaintance with her is concerned. Via Maria we exchange greetings, we hear about each other's minor ailments and major griefs and joys. Maria's sister's house is the place I know Maria goes to most of the times she goes out. But though I have urged her to have her sister come to visit her and me, Maria always replies that her sister is a homebody and does not like to travel.

Maria's interest in my own social life is proud and interested. She is under the impression that I see only the very best people—"the high ups"—but she is rather careful if I am going out to dinner at what she gathers to be a very grand establishment (indicated by my wearing a dinner jacket) that I make a good tea first. "You never get very much to eat at the wealthy people's," she says.

She is also very eager to protect my own dignity and maintain my own status. "We're having a millionaire to lunch today," I said to Maria once. It happened to be true. "We must have a very good lunch," she said; "those people never get enough to eat; I've worked for millionaires. And besides, he mustn't think you can't afford to eat properly."

Again, a lady of my acquaintance had called up in answer to my inquiry as to whether I should wear a white or a black tie, and had left word: "Mr. Edman is to wear a black tie

Thursday night." Maria awaited me that evening, arms
akimbo, to inform me that she had said in just those words
that Dr. Edman knew perfectly well what to wear. But she
has a fixed notion that nobody with anything important to
say says it over the telephone, and her casualness on that
score, especially about names and numbers, is her one im-
perfection. She is, incidentally, more patient with and attentive to gentlemen than to ladies.

Everybody, quite properly, admires Maria's cooking (especially her carrots, about the cooking of which she has a
secret), but she has asked me not to boast about it, as then
people will be disappointed and she will be humiliated. The
chief cross she has to bear is that the digestion of a brain
worker prevents me from letting her give free rein to her art.
She saves that for visitors, and the freest rein she ever gave
was for Father Ford.

I had been telling Maria for some time that Father Ford—
the counsellor to Catholic students at Columbia—was coming to lunch soon. I had never seen any news produce so
electric an effect upon her. For Father Ford, it turned out,
had once been the parish priest at her sister's church, St.
Anne's on Jerome Avenue. And, what was more, she said in
all her years of service she had never yet been in a place
where they had had a priest to lunch.

Usually Maria takes upon herself the problem of the menu.
But, despite the fact that I was often "concentrating" in the
next week, she would appear time and again to announce
some suggested change in the lunch for Thursday. I finally
desperately waived all ability to decide; she was a good Catholic; she should know what priests liked. She was waver-

ing, she said, between grilled chicken and lamb chops with rolled bacon as the principal course.

The day Father Ford was to come to lunch at half-past twelve, I was a little late. I had had a lecture on the Philosophy of Religion from eleven to twelve, and had stopped to argue with a young man named Riley about the origins of Christianity. He was one of Father Ford's protégés, by the way. He had taken the course because Father Ford had told him his faith was not worth very much if it could not stand up against the Department of Philosophy and the Higher Criticism of the Bible.

I came in to find Father Ford seated in that favourite armchair which I have gradually come to realize I can decently use only when I am alone: guests are entitled to its virtues. Father Ford looked very placid and content, and a little amused. I wondered at the amusement.

"I am sorry to be late," I said.

"It's quite all right," he replied; "I have been very well entertained."

We had an excellent and an enormous lunch—grapefruit, timbale of oysters, lamb chops and bacon with three kinds of vegetables, including Maria's specialty—buttered carrots —hearts of lettuce, strawberries and cream—in January— and a cream cake and coffee. There was wine and there was a liqueur; there had been sherry and hors d'œuvre.

About the middle of lunch Father Ford eyed me curiously.

"Do you always have lunch like this?" he asked. "If so, I must steal Maria away for the Newman House."

"No, Father," I said, "this is an obeisance to the Church. I had nothing to do with the ordering of this lunch, and I assure you when I *am* home to lunch I don't get anything like this."

"God looks after you almost as well as if you were one of the faithful," he said.

Father Ford left and I settled down in the easy chair to recuperate from the enormous meal. I began to look over some mail. Maria appeared at the door. She seemed in a fever of restrained excitement.

"Are you concentrating?" she asked.

"No, Maria, I couldn't, not right after that lunch."

"Do you mind if I talk to you, or shall I be disturbing your brains?" (Her regular gambit.)

"I am so glad you came late," she said.

I was surprised at that, for if there is one thing about which Maria will not conceal her displeasure it is my being late when a guest is coming. She was once quite angry with me for two whole days because I had gone out to get some cigarettes and guests had come before I had returned.

"You're glad I came home late, Maria? That's odd, and for a priest, too!"

She beamed and could contain herself no longer. Maria doesn't talk much, but once in a while, in cases of special excitement—like the time she saw somebody jump from a ninth-story window just as she was coming home, or the day the Irish elevator boy told her his wife had had twins—the floodgates are let loose. This was obviously a time of special excitement.

"Well, I must tell you," she said. "Father Ford rang the bell. I opened the door. . . . I said: 'How do you do, Father Ford; I'm so glad you've come. I used to see you in my sister's, St. Anne's Church on Jerome Avenue; and everybody was so fond of you, and the mothers and children cried when you went to Columbia.'

"'But we must go where the Church tells us to,' he said, casting his eyes down.

"'Yes, I know, Father Ford,' I said, 'but the women and children cried anyway. And would you like to see the apartment?' And he said yes. And I showed him the kitchen. And he said: 'What a lovely sunny kitchen!' And he said: 'Professor Edman is one of the best of the younger professors at Columbia.' And I said: 'Yes, I know, and he's so quiet you'd never know he was in the house.' And I showed him the other rooms and the books, and I asked him to sit down and I offered him some sherry, and I told him to make himself quite at home, and I gave him your book on St. Paul. I said you were always thinking about the saints, and I was sure you would end up in the arms of the Church some day, and I am sure you will, too, though everybody's religion is as good as everybody else's, so long as it's his own and he believes it, and is good in his own way. And then you came in, and I'm so glad you came in late, and he did seem to like the lunch. He said so to me when he left.''

"Indeed, he did," I said. "And he wants to steal you for the Newman House."

"Oh, he was only fooling, and it'd be too great a nervous strain to be always working for a priest. But I am glad you came in late."

"Maria," I said, "would you like to take the afternoon off and go up to the Bronx and tell all about this to your sister? You really wouldn't get much done this afternoon."

"I surely would," said Maria.

Maria never enjoyed a guest of mine so much, not even

the friend of mine who, she insists, falsely, looks like Rudy
Vallée.

At my suggestion Maria came to the convocation of Father Ford's new Church of Corpus Christi near Columbia.
Many of us from the university had been invited to attend
in academic garb and march in the procession. The Cardinal
gave his blessing.

That evening I asked Maria how she had liked the cere-
monies.

"Very fine," she said, "and you and Professor C——
looked lovely in the procession."

She thought a moment and looked at me.

"You've received a papal blessing," she said, "do you
know that?"

"Yes," I said.

"Well, you're holy now," she said, and added as she
walked out: "Now be sure to stay that way."

I do not think Maria would mind finding herself in this
book, though she will not read it. She never reads books; she
says they're all alike, and wonders why I keep "poring over"
them. In any case, she cannot mind my writing a little about
one of the kindest and most competent persons I have ever
known, and one with a great gift for happiness who has made
Apartment 9A a wonderful natural basis for ideal flights into
the empyrean with all the comforts of home. She's been
blessed and by more than a Cardinal. And so have I.

SEVENTEEN

Sane Englishmen

To the reading American a first visit to England is not so much one of discovery as of recognition. Everything, not merely literary shrines, seems and is familiar. The thatched and stone houses, the hedges, the soft summer sky, the speech, clipped, musical, and precise, the top hats, the school ties, the pounds, shillings, and pence. There have been intimations of England too since early childhood: *Alice in Wonderland*, Dickens, Gilbert and Sullivan, Jane Austen, 1066, the Magna Charta, Queen Victoria, Piccadilly Circus, Stratford, the towers of Oxford, the guards at Buckingham Palace, the gardens at Kew, the sound of cricket balls on a village green or croquet on the smooth lawn of an historic country house. In schooldays one is fed (or used to be) on Washington Irving's *Bracebridge Hall,* and, despite the repeated revolt against colonialism (from Lowell's essay "On a Certain Condescension in Foreigners" down), the literary American is early and oddly nostalgic for England. Or, at any rate, so was the author of these pages.

I can hardly remember when I first longed to go to

England or when I for the first time met an Englishman. But by the time I was a senior in college, the image of England as a green and pleasant land was fixed in my imagination, and fixed, too, was the picture of Englishmen as human paragons, fair-spoken, clean-limbed, polite and poetic—above all quiet paragons. Thus had I by the time I had received my college degree (and long before I had visited England) come to conjure up the standard model of that ruling—or once ruling—race.

I should know better by this time. I have certainly met enough eccentric, stupid, rude Englishmen not to be taken in by the legend of the English as invariably normal, sensible, even-tempered, courteous, and sensitive. I know, or should know, that this stereotype is a myth which artful propaganda has imposed on the English-speaking world, which it has indeed imposed as well on a good deal of the world that speaks other languages. It is the legend assiduously cultivated, I am prepared to believe, and deviously propagated by the British Foreign Office in pursuance of the dubious ends and circuitous means of British imperial policy.

I am aware, moreover, that "mad" is the standard epithet for Englishmen all over the Continent. Only mad Englishmen go out in the noonday sun in summer in Rome; only mad Englishmen, with the exception of a few madder Germans (as the natives will assure you), go swimming in the chilly February of the South of France. Only madmen could have invented the term "His Majesty's Loyal Opposition." Sane people would never dream of dressing for dinner at a remote Alpine hotel six thousand feet high, where they have come for a summer holiday. Sensible persons would not tolerate English food, boil all the flavour out of vegetables, maltreat coffee out of recognition, drive on the wrong side of the road, swallow half their syllables in speaking, insist on speaking English to foreigners and talking it twice as loudly when the foreigner presumably out of stubbornness or stupidity will not understand.

I know all that. I have entertained myself and sometimes my friends with tales of English oddities. Yet I cannot get over my feeling or escape the residual impression from all the meetings and friendships I have had with Englishmen in England, in the United States, and on the Continent, that English men are sane (I know less about English women).

I cannot rest until I have tried to put down some of the things that have led me to that impression and I think have led many Americans to it. English sanity may be one of the world's illusions; the very charm of the myth may be its danger. Since for better or worse that illusion persists in many quarters, the natural history of it in one academic Anglophile may not be without interest to other bemused victims. Perhaps if one could analyse the charm of the English, one could exorcize their power.

The chief thing, I suppose, that early led or misled me, when I did finally come to England as a young instructor on a *Wanderjahr,* was the Englishman's quiet speech and understatement, true practically of all classes of society except a few fashionables whose loud speech ostentatiously and feudally ignores the presence of their neighbours in restaurants. I still recall my first vivid impression of English calm. It came when I was crossing to England after a year on the Continent. One cannot arrive at a French port without a sense that the people there to meet the ship have never before had the experience of seeing one arrive. The event seems not only unprecedented but almost calamitous. Things get done eventually despite all the flurry and bustle, the shouting, the altercations, the torrents of speech. The customs men examine, the passengers find their compartments, the train gets off, and on time. But after what communal hysteria! The same situation recurs when one is leaving France. One would think it were the last ship that was ever going to leave; it seems a piece of good luck to be on it.

Matthew Arnold's lines on "Dover Beach" sang in my head when I first saw the cliffs of Dover.

> *The sea is calm to-night,*
> *The tide is full, the moon lies fair*
> *Upon the straits;—on the French coast the light*
> *Gleams and is gone; the cliffs of England stand*
> *Glimmering and vast, out in the tranquil bay.*

But even before that I was already in England, on the calm Channel boat, among the quiet tones of the officers and crew. At Dover there was a tranquil customs examination, a polite deferential murmur about things to declare, wines, spirits, jewels, silks, and tobacco. There were the quiet fellow-passengers, the noiseless serving of tea, the train sliding almost silently out of the station at Dover and as silently and smoothly coming to a halt at Victoria. There were the subdued porters and the peaceful hotel in London, right off the bustle of Regent Street. Nothing seemed urgent or pressing or excessive. One seemed to have stepped by a miracle into a world of moderation, of good sense, of unobtrusive good manners, of peace.

I have been told by many people, including well-informed

Englishmen, that I must not be misled by these urbane surfaces of daily life in England. I have been reminded that I must not mistake the public-school manner of the upper-class Englishman or the traditional deference of the English servant or tradesman for sanity. It has been pointed out to me, and I have, without help, noticed time and again what a mass of repressions and sentimentalities (and brutalities as well) lie behind the public-school mask, what bitterness often and seeds of revolt in the deference of the English servant or worker or tradesman. I recall, too, that the most interesting Englishmen have often been mad or have been so regarded by their fellow-countrymen. English sanity, I am reminded and often unpleasantly constrained to remember, is often merely English stodginess and conventionality, the latter, to anybody but an Englishman, often absurd enough. All that is true, perhaps, and yet the impression of English sense and of English sensibility persists and the illustrations of it crowd into my memory.

I had started out from Oxford on a solitary cycling trip. It began to rain an hour after I had started. I decided to stay for the night at the little inn in the market-place at Abingdon. I had an English country hotel dinner which might certainly have been a little more mad without hurt to itself. The normality of an anonymous thick soup, of boring mutton, of respectable boiled potatoes, of a moral enough gooseberry tart, left something to be desired. I had, moreover, been fed on that unvarying tradition for weeks. I was sitting in the hotel lounge, looking out into the old market square. It had finally stopped raining and in the late summer dusk the lamps had just been lighted and gleamed on the still wet pavement. The tall, quiet, collected-looking, bald-headed, middle-aged man who had been sipping his whisky and soda in silence for the last half-hour, was looking out at the pavement, too.

"That," he said without preamble, "would be harder to paint than it looks."

"I imagine it would," I said, a little surprised. "Are you a painter?"

"I paint a little," he replied, and turned to look at the pavement again. I thought of the Englishman I had once met in Assisi who, when I happened to mention Etruscan inscriptions in the region, said casually that he had written a little book on the subject. I looked it up a few months later in the British Museum. It turned out to be a large two-volume work and, in so far as there could be a definitive work on that mysterious theme, here it certainly was. I wondered if this were possibly a Royal Academician, or, even more interesting, a rebel from the Royal Academy. We began to talk about painting, about music, about the nature of art itself, about America, about England, about the League of Nations. It grew late. We turned to art again and broke a lance on the subject of Cézanne, he claiming that that painter was much over-rated. I grew more and more curious as to who my companion was. If he *was* a painter, he seemed singularly well informed on politics and economics. Painting seemed, as the evening wore on, to be revealed as his consuming interest. Yet I could have sworn he was not a painter by profession.

"I spend my holidays painting a little," he said as we parted. "You must come to see us when you are in London." Some time later I spent a weekend with him and his family in a house filled with Tudor furniture in which he specialized; another of his hobbies was eighteenth-century literature, especially minor poets. He talked to me a good deal of the League of Nations Union, in which he was an active worker. He seemed to find time, besides, for being very busy in a flourishing though modest wine trade. He referred to his job, as I have heard many Englishmen do, as his berth. He wished he could take longer holidays, for it was fun to paint. He must go back to Abingdon some time and try to paint that market-place by lamplight just after a rain.

I know, of course, and knew then that there are business men in America who like to paint, who collect old furniture and who love old books, and business men in England who are duller Babbitts, but I chance never to have met anyone quite like Mr. Broadbent, with his modest expertness, his self-deprecating connoisseurship, his unself-conscious citizenship of a world of beauty in which he imaginatively lived and to which in a small, unpretentious way he tried to make his contribution. Either England is filled with such people or some accident of destiny has brought an unusually large number of them into my orbit. There is Mr. E——, the busy lawyer in London, who translates the Byzantines, for whom he had acquired a love at St. Paul's School. There is Sir Edward —— who, in intervals from work at the Admiralty, managed to make himself an amateur scholar on Greek ruins in Sicily and on Wordsworth and Goethe as well. There is the Civil Servant who writes light verse and edits Elizabethan plays. The tradition goes back to Austin Dobson in the London Post Office and to Pepys at the Admiralty, with his not inconsiderable knowledge of and feeling for music and plays. One used to hear Germans scoff at English scholarship because, even when it was professional, it retained the character of the amateur, not simply in manner but in fact. One hears tales at Oxford of how Jowett, the translator of Plato (with the help of Swinburne and of his students), used to thunder against "research" at Oxford. The amenities of pleasantly casual and, to a scholar, unpleasantly inaccurate conversation at an English country house can become wearying, and the urbane habit of easy or epigrammatic conversation at Oxford can fail to become scholarship. The amateur scholar gentleman can easily become the expert amateur thief of other people's time. But to an American used to seeing scholarship itself become an intense competitive business, to seeing professors of literature with, at best, an archæological professional interest in the dates of a man's texts rather than the art which made him important, it is a relief to observe the easy browsing among delightful pastures of the mind by the merchants and the civil servants of England. It is a relief, too, to see men who can be interested in the arts without being arty, and collectors for their own delight rather than for panoply and parade. I seem to have met in England, more than anywhere else I have been, people not content to be *Nibelungen* living for ever underground but predisposed to come up now and again to breathe the bright upper air.

I have been misled (what American has not?), I confess, by the habit of deprecation, of understatement, of avoidance of any emphasis or even frankness of avowal of some passionate interest or central concern. "There are," an English friend explained to me one June day at Oxford, "two unpardonable sins at Oxford, one is to be *seen* working, the other is to be enthusiastic." I had observed how people working hard for a prize would never give work as an excuse for declining an invitation to tea or to tennis. I once walked away from a lecture by Gilbert Murray—attended by a scattered two dozen or so—with an undergraduate of eighteen, who said scarcely a word. "How did you like the lecture?" I asked. I had been moved, as I had been when I had heard Murray in America, by the poetic sympathy, the liberal vision and imagination, of this ambassador of the ancient Greeks. "His textual criticism," the undergraduate said, "was fair enough, his humanism was bloody awful." I had heard people at Oxford explain why so many brilliant scholarly careers begun there in youth evaporated into nothingness by middle age. "What is the use," a world-weary don remarked, "of publishing anything at Oxford? There will simply be seven hundred people heard to remark in boredom that a semicolon is misplaced."

The habit of deprecation extends to the very young, out of the fear, doubtless, of being thought to take serious things too seriously; part of the public-school tradition, where even the masters are a little suspicious of those pupils who take their studies rather than their games *au grand sérieux;* the same thing, doubtless, that makes an English schoolboy a little ashamed of having too French a French accent. Certainly by the time many of these young men come to Oxford, the temper of casualness or affected casualness is pronounced. There is one *locus classicus* in my memory. F. C. S. Schiller, the *enfant terrible* of Oxford philosophy, the pragmatist among the Brahmins, had invited me to an undergraduate philosophy club—the Sunflower Club, I believe—one Sunday evening at Merton College. An undergraduate had read an extraordinarily well-informed paper on William

James. It sounded surprising enough to hear that arch-unorthodox thinker defended in this arch-orthodox seat of the classical tradition. The young reader brought to his apologia for an exuberant American thinker all the aplomb and forensic dexterity familiar at the Oxford Union. His paper in turn was devastatingly commented upon by another member of the club, a youth apparently very well trained in all the dialectic arts so familiar in that bible of Oxford philosophy, F. H. Bradley's *Appearance and Reality,* and gifted with gaiety besides. I found myself at the close of the meeting talking to the two young men who, despite the vehemence of the critic, were apparently good friends. I said I should like to see more of such lovers—and haters—of William James. Would they come to tea?

When a professor of philosophy in America invites two talented young students of philosophy to tea, he expects, and they expect, that the talk will be about philosophy. I thought that before we had finished the first cup we should be deep in a discussion of a pluralistic universe, and I should have these two philosophical fighting cocks again at each other. It was the fourth cup, and, though I had essayed the subject, philosophy was far from coming to a boil. I could scarcely believe it was the same two undergraduates. The mention of William James evoked but the faintest glimmer of recognition. There was no evidence that these two had ever heard of philosophy. There were desultory comments on rowing and on gardening, reflections on high teas consumed in Scotland on holiday trips in the past, polite canvassing of the merits of China and India tea. There were no attempts at the epigrams of the other night or of its dialectic. Not until the tea things were cleared away did I begin to recognize my two philosophers of the Sunflower Club. Only after the fifth cigarette did both the philosophical passion and dialectical skill which had so impressed me the previous Sunday make their reappearance. The orthodox youth had not been indulging in mere forensics and raillery the other night; it seemed to him that, unless you believed in one rational system of the universe, both your life and your morality were paralysed. The youth who defended James had found in his "open universe" a liberation from the tight world of thought in which at Oxford he had been confined. The two antagonists went at each other with skill and fervour. And they both apologized for the fervour when they rose to go.

Over and over again in England I had and have since noticed what surely constitutes part of the charm of English manners and the puzzling irritation, to an American or to a Continental, of English character and possibly, therefore, of British policy. The atmosphere of English casualness is most attractive. It is pleasant to see things done without fuss. It is engaging to meet a man (as I once did in Naples) who will casually discuss Plato's *Republic* for an hour and then indolently rise and announce: "I must push on; my boat leaves for India in half an hour." It is agreeable to see railway terminals with little excitement or confusion, to see policemen standing about in Hyde Park in good-natured insouciance while orators announce the end of the world or of the British Empire. It is delightful to hear tales of the General Strike in 1926 (when class bitterness came as near rending England as it ever has done), how the policemen played cricket with the strikers, how crowds amusedly and encouragingly watched dukes handle motorbuses. It is cheerful to see a postman (a little too loaded down with packages, one would say) announce to a clerk in a bank: "His Majesty's Government come to call upon you!" Again after the turbulent American adjectives of enthusiasm one enjoys hearing things, plays, books, music, described as "not too bad," instead of as "marvellous" or "divine." It is comfortable to be among quiet, unhurried voices, talking without intensity at tea over the thin slices of bread and butter in the hazy sunlight of a summer afternoon in the Cotswolds or in a winter dusk, gathered around a cosy, unspectacular little fire.

Surely I have not been the first to fall victim to this atmosphere of the pleasantly muted, soft casualness of English life. Nor am I, I am sure, the first to be often annoyed by it, as well as perplexed. If it is pleasant to be without fuss, surely on the other hand there are things worth making a fuss for or against or over. I have a collector's passion for books about England, especially those by foreigners. One of the most engaging and penetrating of them is that written by an enlightened Dutch journalist who had for twenty years lived in London. *The English, Are They Human?* Dr. Renier called his book. One soon divines that all this quiet restraint is not human. The restraint of the well-bred upper-class Englishman comes to seem inhuman affectation or inhuman conformity; the quiet of the English poor super-human or infra-human patience.

I have at various times been conquered or annoyed by the restraint of the well-bred, well-placed Englishman, by that almost universal habit of deprecation, for instance, engaging enough when it is not itself a form of conceit and a precaution against giving one's self away. (For I do not need to be reminded that there are conceited Englishmen; I have spent too much time in Oxford, London, and English country houses not to know it.) That pleasant chap with whom one was a fellow-guest at a weekend, or chatted with in a lounge at a club, and whom one wishes one might come to know better; I have known many such Englishmen. I seldom came to know them better even when I had known them long. What is more, I do not think anyone ever came to know them much better, possibly not even they themselves. For the quiet passion for passionlessness, the lust for good form, for not doing or saying the outrageous or excessive thing, has often enough a depressing consequence. It not infrequently solidifies into the habit of saying nothing of any interest or depth or importance, and of saying and feeling nothing at all. I have an incorrigible weakness for the grace of the English manner. But how often I have been wearied by the well-bred triviality, the decent correctness, the niceness of English tea-table conversation, the stolidity of the faces mostly hidden behind newspapers in the morning trains, the menacing silences at English family breakfasts, the stuffiness of the talk after dinner, with or without the ladies. It is not for nothing, I gathered after a while, that English poets have so often fled their school, their university, or their country. I began to understand why Englishmen returning from New York feel, as one of them put it to me, as if he had been living on champagne and fresh air. And I have still to meet a sensitive Englishman who has not, if I have known him long enough, begun to talk about the devastation that the public-school system has wrought upon the spontaneities of English character. Englishmen know their own souls best, and since even in the confessional mood they manage to keep their own counsel, I have not been able to discover just how much damage the habit of correctness in deportment has done them, or how much actual suffering it has imposed. Yet if the genteel tradition in England has stultified many mute Miltons, some of them, a rather surprising number, have survived and come to public birth.

It is especially hard to say what interior tensions and unhappiness have been caused by the regimen of observing the social rules. Occasionally one catches hints:

My friend M—— T—— is a cultivated engineer in one of the large English semi-public services. He has all the competence and conscience for which the leaders in these are famous. We were discussing the themes broached in the above paragraph on our way back to our hotel in the South of France, where we were staying among a leisure-class English colony. We had spent the afternoon and much of the evening at a little medieval town perched on the mountains back of the Côte d'Azur. We had dined at an obscure café where, before the potage had been served, everyone was talking gaily to everyone else, and everyone present (every French person) had joined in the singing that had been begun suddenly by the proprietor, soon joined by his wife as she was dispensing drinks behind the counter. We came back to the hotel lounge and found some fifteen or twenty English people sedately staring at each other in stony curiosity and mistrust. "Don't English people ever let themselves go, even on the Continent?" I asked. "No," he said, "not really, except when they may make a special point of it, as part of the obligation of a Continental holiday. Restraint is bred in us very early. But, do you know, sometimes," he added suddenly and wistfully, "the strain is rather severe." I have heard other Englishmen confess as much. I have time and again been provoked to wonder what depths of fermenting unhappiness or of stifled joy have lain below the externals, at once so rigid and so smooth, of well-bred English life. As a water-diviner can sense the presence of water in apparently dry regions, so one can often sense in Englishmen these subterranean reservoirs of pain or of delight. In genius it breaks through into lyric poetry and, as Santayana remarks somewhere: "There is a poet in the heart of every nice Englishman." In *nearly* every one, perhaps. Sometimes the impeccable surface comes to be all that there is, as if there never had been anything else. It took me, incorrigible Anglophile, many years to discover that, in the smooth flow of English speech, there might be nothing but polite clichés, little more than nothingness or nonsense, so standard that they seemed, at least to the English, to make sense. Sometimes the suppressed individuality of feeling or thought may burst out into eccentricities of thought or conduct or perhaps only of clothes. Where but in England could there be so many fanatic small causes, such weird little backwaters and revolts from the established pattern of upper middle-class life, such Dickensian pictures walking on London streets, even in the Season, and on English lanes. Every English village may not have its village idiot, but I am by this time convinced that every English family has its special odd number who flourishes in singular ways. Sometimes the streak of nonsense or of oddity flourishes to the point of genius, as in *Alice in Wonderland;* a passionate nonconformity may, while outwardly conforming (was not Lewis Carroll a proper English don?), utter itself in a superb absurdity. Then the English canonize it and take it to their bosoms. Sometimes the flame, repressed by good form, breaks through into passionate beauty. The Englishman builds a high hedge around his private heart, as he builds a hedge around his garden. Often when one is allowed to peer over the hedge or enter the garden, one finds strange or beautiful flowers there.

But the habit of correctness, displaying itself in depreciation, in understatement, in an avoidance of the hysterical, has one spiritual consequence that qualifies its initial appeal and poisons its charm. It was not long before I discovered how in England, as elsewhere—but in England particularly because there insouciance is a fetish—casualness so easily turns into callousness and into lack of seriousness. I was not in England very long for the first time before I discovered how the most decent people among the economically secure in England can be casual to the point of brutality with respect to those outside the charmed circle. There are many urbane groups in England among whom it is still considered impolite or fantastic or crotchety to notice, or above all to mention, the shocking conditions of labour among the English servants or of unemployment in the "special areas" (itself a characteristic euphemism) of South Wales or Northern England. One should be kind to the poor as one should be kind to animals (except the fox). Every English gentleman knows that and is or supposes he is that. But there are relatively liberal quarters where I have found that it is regarded as vulgarly eccentric or indecently Left to question the social and industrial misery and poverty which support the amenities and dignities of English life as lived by the few. There are Common Rooms in Oxford and drawing-rooms in country houses where (I am surely not the first to testify to it) kindliness, courtesy, intelligence, and wit flourish. But one would hardly gather from conversations in them that much water had flowed under the mill since the eighteenth century and that that water is now rising to a flood.

Even the threat of war, though it is now on every Englishman's mind, must not be taken too seriously or at least talked about too seriously. Gas masks are sold in the chemists' shops; there is genuine alarm about not impossible air raids, for England is no longer an island. But Air Raid Protection is still something to joke about, and will be so when it is no longer a laughing matter. But one day, while brooding these matters, it occurred to me by the same token the English are safe against Fascism. One could hardly imagine a dictator being taken seriously in this country so terrified of rhetoric and exaggeration. Perhaps the English habit of not taking things too seriously has its ultimate values after all. Or perhaps that is just what the dictators on the Continent are counting on.

The inhuman pattern of English upper-class life used to puzzle this bemused observer less than the patience of the English poor. The good-natured endurance of the English underprivileged, of the shockingly ill-clothed, ill-nourished and ill-fed of the East End of London or of the industrial North, has always seemed to me one of the pitiful wonders of the world. What has made half the fame of Cockney speech, itself ugly, is not its rough way with consonants, its quaint transformation of vowels into diphthongs, but the equally cynical good nature of the Cockney temperament. I have still to find an ill-natured Cockney in London. But seeing the inhabitants of the mean streets of London, and the squalid ways in which people live in villages and on farms, so tranquil and old-world to the traveller's eye,

I have wondered how they manage to endure it with so much kindliness and goodwill. I think I know now. The patience of the English poor is a correlate to the class assumptions of the English rich. It is a leftover or hangover of the feudal tradition, and even the entrenched rich are beginning to find, if only from the speeches of His Majesty's Loyal Opposition, that the assumptions of the rich are not held by everybody in England to be eternal. But the surface of the leisure-class tradition endures even among the poor who no longer share the assumptions which generated it. I am convinced that a Cockney executioner would say "Sir" to the lords he was liquidating. Perhaps the reason a revolution is not nearer in England is that even the burdened poor in England do not like hurry or fuss, but like even necessary change to be made with dignity.

It was at first extraordinarily pleasant and reassuring in England to be taken for a gentleman, until I found out that that is not a compliment to one's self but a stereotype reaction to a class, a class with money to spend. Once many years ago a friend and I took a cycling trip through the English countryside, itself a wonderful perambulant introduction to English poetry. We decided we were going to try to know the people of the countryside as we wandered through it, and in the interest of this human exploration as well as of economy we stayed at little "pubs" on the outskirts of small villages. We drank beer with the local farmers. It was no use, so far as a sense of oneness, a Tolstoyan union, with the common man was concerned. We were earmarked as gentlemen; that is, we were not workers. There was a bar of deference that made it as impossible to give and take freely as if we were dukes, instead of young Americans on tour.

I have heard English gentlemen, that is people with a "public-school" background, give a reasoned and plausible defence of the English leisure-class tradition. The aristocratic pattern sets a tone for the whole of England and its good manners, its sense of *noblesse oblige,* percolates through the whole population. It is a pretty theory, and I am prepared to believe there is something in it. It is agreeable to think of the squire as of a shepherd looking after his tenantry and setting a model for their manners and morals, having as his business in life the exhibition of a type of excellence to be both emulated and served. Indeed I know one recent graduate of Cambridge so taken with that idea that he has settled down to the noble old house he has inherited and at the age of thirty has become the magistrate, the churchwarden, the pillar of his village. He is a conscientious public servant and as a model of good manners could not be improved upon. Dante's conception of the souls in heaven, each in his own radiating sphere of excellence, could hardly have a nobler sound than his own conception of his function. But the Industrial Revolution has not arrived in heaven, and even before the Industrial Revolution, one gathers, not all English gentlemen were completely dominated by the ideals of good manners and *noblesse oblige.* Nor are they so now.

An English friend went so far as to explain to me with great persuasiveness (when I happened to express my astonishment that the English with their tenderness for animals still did not mind cruelty to the fox) that it was the sporting tradition that had made English character at its best, the world not of games, but the world of racing, fishing, and hunting. He clearly saw its absurdities, as well as its beauties, for he had been brought up to it in his own family, where only he was an intellectual truant from the tradition. That world had bred the pleasure of a game without competitiveness; it had bred kindliness, courtesy, and the sense of *noblesse oblige* in its members. The Battle of Waterloo may have been won on the playing-fields of Eton, but the integrity and the courtesy of the English gentleman was the traditional chivalry of the chase, the product of the love of fine horses trained for the race course and of the courage and judgment and physical fitness needed by the rider in the hunting field. Ascot, for all its parade of fashion, was a festival of this aristocracy, combining the ladies' garden party with the sporting field. You might say what you would about the narrowness of the sporting set; there was much of poetry and mind that never came into their ken, and their world was bounded by England or something vaguely subsidiary called the Empire. But if I wished to understand English character, my friend said, I must live in the old houses it lived in, and meet some of its finest products, some of whom inhabited now and again the British Foreign Office. Pressed, my friend admitted some blots on their escutcheon. He was not prepared to defend British foreign policy—it was not always sporting—and was ready to admit that the sporting world of England, with the vanishing of the big estates, was not going to last for ever. But if I was to comprehend England I must understand the Ascot race meet as well as the Glyndebourne Music Festival; if I was to comprehend English character in its simplicity and directness and decencies, unbemused by ideas (ideas always fuddled the English, he assured me), I must realize that much of English character came, even among Englishmen who never dreamed of hunting and fishing and racing, from the set which for generations had been preoccupied by those enterprises. The man who assured me of these things went to Glyndebourne as well as to Ascot and had other books in his library than *Burke's Peerage* and *Debrett;* he read the *New Statesman* as well as *Country Life.*

From the world my friend said gave the stamp to English character it is a far cry to the world I heard about from a Labour editor and from a professor at the London School of Economics. Every year or so in New York, Harold Laski used to talk to a group at the home of a mutual friend and tell of the ebb and flow of the tide toward the co-operative commonwealth in England. In the *Manchester Guardian,* too, one received a different picture of England from that painted at Oxford or in an ancient baronial hall. What Manchester thinks today—I know the old slogan—England will think tomorrow. But Manchester has been thinking for a hundred years now, and there are echoes of yesterday all over England, even among the people who are thinking about tomorrow. Millions of people in England who never come anywhere near Ascot and Oxford are thinking about tomorrow, and with as much bitterness as is possible to English character. I was forcibly reminded of this once because of being delayed by a fog, not in England but in New York harbour. Our ship had come to Quarantine too late to be examined by the customs. We were going to remain at anchor all night.

"Too bad for both the passengers and crew," I remarked to the polite, silent young steward in charge of my cabin.

"It doesn't matter about the crew, sir," he remarked with an unmistakable tinge of bitterness. "The last thing to be considered, sir, in the British mercantile marine is the crew. You haven't seen the living-quarters for the crew on this ship, sir." He described dryly the crowding, the lack of adequate sanitation, the bad and scanty food. "And it's a new ship, sir, only four years old."

"How does everybody manage to remain so cheerful and polite?" I asked.

"We're cheerful and polite to the passengers, sir. We're not quite so cheerful with each other. We have a greeting when we meet, though. We say at the worst things: 'Are you happy in your work?' But it's what my job is worth to be talking like this. And there are fifty fools waiting at Southampton for my job. Romance of the sea! Bloody nonsense, sir.

"And," he continued (it was the time of the Abyssinian crisis), "by the time we get back to Southampton, we'll probably be at war with Italy. And for what? For the old boys of the public schools of England! *They* run the banks and the shipping companies and all. And I and all of us will be asked to fight for two shillings a day, and for what? The public schoolboys of England are quarrelling with the public schoolboys of Italy, or whatever they call public schoolboys there, for gold and oil and banks. Abyssinia is the least of it. By the time I get back to Southampton there will be posters all over: 'Your King and Country Need You.' And now with the wireless and all that, there'll probably be loudspeakers on the motor lorries, and you'll hear the stuff blasted at you wherever you go. And what's more, I'll probably be impressed and taken in by it, and so will thousands like me. The capitalist class is very clever. They know all the answers, or if they don't, they're clever enough to find those who do. Shall I call you at eight, sir?"

It is a long way from the fashionable crowds at Ascot to the crew's quarters on a British ship and from the country-gentleman tradition to the bitterness and discontent finding its voice for me by accident in an articulate cabin steward. But it finds its voice not only in the safety valve of the orators at Hyde Park, threatening the liquidation of the Tories while the polite Bobbies stand unconcerned. It is finding its voice in the House of Commons as well. But (though Marxists be at my throat for saying so) I have a persistent sense from acquaintance with many kinds and classes of Englishmen that, by some alchemy unknown to Marxism, the classes in England are as English as they are classes, and my bitter steward, my country gentleman friend, my engineer, the Oxford undergraduates, the orators at Hyde Park and the policemen, the dons in the Common Room, the farmers in the local pub, were all more English than they were anything else and bound together by that odd tie, indefinable and inexpungeable.

My friend and (I cannot resist it) former student, Jacques Barzun, has written a book to show that national as well as racial traits are myths. In the light of the uprush of superstitions about both these things that threatens to destroy European civilization, I am glad he is so convincing. But at the risk of being included in his anthology of inanities on the subject in some future revision of his book, I make bold to discern some persistent English traits, discernible, no doubt, in the way that all Chinese look alike to those who do not know them very well. What one detects, Dr. Barzun assures us, if one alleges to detect national traits, are not really national or racial; they are the functions of culture patterns. I am content to believe that it is a culture pattern, the impact of a tradition, the interest on inherited values, that makes the English quality. But it is a quality that one over and over again recognizes in Englishmen of widely varying classes and interests, spiritual and economic. And it *is* a quality, if quality is that which one feels immediately, an authentic signature to utterance, an unmistakable temper and tempo in action. I do not pretend to be historian or anthropologist enough to give its natural history. I can testify only to having sensed it and I know I am not the only American who has done so. Perhaps my gentleman from the country is right, and some of it comes from the percolation of the English aristocratic tradition that still persists through or despite all the apparatus of democracy and all the transformations of industrialism. The traces of that influence are everywhere. It is not evidenced simply in the fact that the cabin steward in the midst of his bitter utterances still said "Sir." It is rather that one felt in him a sense of English things, and of England, affinity to English soil and to English feelings and to the traditional English pattern of living. Even in his violence there was a certain moderation, a reasonableness in his attempt at understanding the circumstances which had made his plight and might even make it worse, an awareness of the tradition in which his plight was rooted. That reasonableness of the English temperament can sometimes be exasperating. It accepts with genial stoicism or with urbane smugness things as they are. By things as they are and as they must be it means too frequently the ways, insular and narrow enough, of traditional English society, a feudalism persisting under the forms of democracy and in the conflicts of an industrial age. Reasonableness in action means often enough simply compromise, the middle way of some immediate solution that at once avoids and creates further problems. It is a kind of muddled eclecticism in theory, and

a rough and ready empiricism, at once tolerant and superficial, like the thought of John Locke. Whether in metaphysics or in dealing with dictators, finalities are avoided,
just as ultimate things must not be discussed at tea-time, or
ecstasy or exact doctrine required or indeed permitted at a
Sunday service or from a bishop. The English mind, like the
English weather on a fair June day, is gentle and pleasant,
but its blue skies are softly flecked with clouds. Its fields are
green, but they are hedged. So too the English church service has, save at its exceptional best, formal grace and decorous beauty without being mystical or profound or intense.
But poetry has thrived in these hedged fields, and poets have
been prompted to say ineffable things under these variable
and misty skies. The tempered good sense and muted poetry
crop up in all varieties and classes of Englishmen, and I have
felt it in dons and street-sweepers, in squires and farmers, in
cities and villages, in bank managers and postmen, in bus-
drivers and bishops in England. The good sense is often
tempered to an extreme by insularity and the poetry muted
altogether by decorum. But it is there and not only in the
shadow of Magdalen Tower or in conversation at the Athen-
æum or in the writings of John Stuart Mill. It crops up in the
comment of a Devon farmer on the weather or of a policeman on the crowds.

"No Englishman could be so fond of England," an English friend once remarked to me, as I, an American, joined in
prose a long line of English poets who had sung in praise of
England. "No Englishman would say he was," I replied, "or
perhaps only English poets would do so."

If it is a myth, this England that lingers in my memory,
it is a myth that is one of the reassuring illusions of a good

part of the English-speaking world. It is an image of sense and sensibility that, whatever its history or its effects or its future (since its foundations are crashing), I should hate to see pass not only from my memory but from the world. If the co-operative commonwealth is to come anywhere, it would be pleasant to see it retain the qualities that, though a long way this side of Paradise, English life has, at its best, among its green hedged fields and among people like these with a capacity for simple things and quiet content. I once had as host the Professor of Poetry at Oxford who said he guarded against insularity by spending his holidays abroad. "But do you know," he added, "when I set foot on Dover, I feel I am among sane people again?" I have sometimes felt the same, landing at Southampton; and I have shuddered to think, walking a field path in the Cotswolds and hearing an aeroplane overhead, how insanity across the North Sea, or compromise or muddle-headedness in London, might to-gether cause this island of reasonableness to vanish from the world. That reasonableness is not the *raison* of the French, but the "reasonableness" of human accommodation, and aware-ness of the limits of logic in human affairs, where conse-quences in logic are not always consequences in fact.

The passing of the British Empire, with all its parade and power, may not be the world's loss; the passing of "this demi-Eden" would be such. For other virtues, other lands; and I have always been happy to come home, but bringing the myth or the image with me—in the midst of New York some time, gulping lunch at a soda fountain, remembering tea before an English fire, or the fleecy clouds over Dart-moor on a summer day.

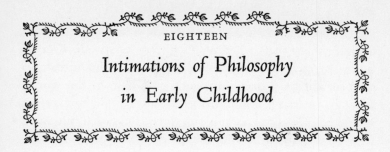

EIGHTEEN

Intimations of Philosophy
in Early Childhood

IT IS possible, I suspect, for most people at all interested
in philosophy to put their finger on the time and the
book that first introduced them to the "subject." Philosophy
in my own mind will always be associated with Bakewell's
Source Book in Ancient Philosophy, which contains fragments
remaining from the early Greeks: Thales, Anaximander,
Heraclitus, and Empedocles. The names themselves sounded
like incantations. I had an early impression (from which I
have not yet recovered) that Greek philosophers in the Ionian
Peninsula for some strange reason *wrote* in fragments. As a
freshman, too, I vaguely had the idea that Bakewell had
with his own hands gathered together these fragments at
Yale, or had composed them there, and that the learned professor was himself somehow the source of Greek philosophy.
I shall also associate my first bookish relations with philosophy with that great grey volume, translated from unintel-
ligible German into formidable English: Paulsen's *Introduction to Philosophy.* There I gathered that philosophy consisted
of an astounding number of isms, with innumerable sub-

isms, and that somewhere in that ismatic jungle lay the Truth. Finally, by myself, outside of class, I discovered the little yellow book in the Home University Library, J. A. Thomson's *Introduction to Science,* which opened up the various branches of knowledge and their interrelations and made me feel that with sufficient time and diligence I could become one of the masters—in outline—of all that was to be known.

But there is a moment, or kind of moment, harder to identify. It occurs usually, I suspect, before one knows what the word "philosophy" is, or when one vaguely associates the word "philosophical" with Red Indians burning in stubborn and dignified fortitude at the stake, or with a man watching the ruins and embers of his house, or hearing of the death or elopement of his wife, with grave serenity. Some experience, some word, or some odd fancy crossing one's inexperienced mind—and one is in the presence of, and feels, the delicious, puzzling incitement (without knowing either phrase) of philosophical issues and ultimate things. I have friends who occasionally report instances of such early speculative awakening in their small children, and I know that, from John Locke down, the baby has been a favourite illustration of philosophers—the baby putting together the colour and sound and taste and smell and feel of an orange and saying: "Lo! it is an object, it is an orange!"

Being childless, I have only the smallest stock of illustrations of this philosophical awakening among children, though I gather from my friends that their infant sons are all metaphysicians. I know, for instance, that Ian, aged nine, reads Gibbon, and I hear from his father that his mind is as sceptical and circumspect as that of Hume. I did once take a walk with a child who asked suddenly:"Who made the world?" For the sake of brevity I replied: "God." "Who made God?" was the next question. To reply that God was a First Cause, the Uncreated Creator of all things seemed a stiff dose for a child and would only bring on further questions. I said I would tell him later. But for the awakening of the philosophical impulse in children I can only refer to one autobiographical instance, and I shall try to keep out of my remembrance such sophisticated gloss as a later education in philosophy gave me. I am convinced, as I look back, that all the great issues, Freedom and Determinism, God, Immortality, the reality of the external world, and the nature of reality itself, are first stumbled upon when one is very young. I can even imagine that some day a psychiatrist will prove that speculative interests are early childhood fixations and that the metaphysician is an infant trailing clouds of inglorious complexes from the nursery.

Time is certainly the pet theme of much contemporary thought, and I had as certainly not read the modern physicists or Einstein's early work at the age of thirteen. But it was then, if I remember, that I myself first hit upon that perplexity, current in philosophy since Plato defined Time as the moving picture of eternity, a phrase itself puzzle enough. I remember one day coming to my older sister and saying I was bothered about Time. She was, as she is still, full of sound sense and human perception and has never allowed herself to be distracted by nonsense, however elaborate and imposing. She is a philosopher free from cobwebs.

"What do you mean," she said, "you are bothered by time?"

"Well," I said, "take today, for instance. It's really here right now, this very minute, for instance, isn't it?"

"Yes, of course," she said, and turned back to the piano on which she was playing one-half of Beethoven's *Fifth Symphony* arranged for four hands.

"But wait a minute," I said, "tomorrow today will be yesterday, won't it? It will be gone. And tomorrow is not here yet, and it really *isn't* at all. It's all very puzzling. What *is* Time?"

"Time for you to go to bed," she said briskly and, refusing to be entangled any further in aerie irrelevance and childishness, she turned back again to the Andante.

I did go to bed, but I did not sleep. For I was obsessed by the awful unreality of something I had hitherto taken for granted. There was, I mused, last summer on the Jersey coast—the long summer afternoons, the tang of the salt spray as the breakers broke round one as one waded into the surf, the agreeable burning warmth of the sun as one basked on the beach. But *that* was last summer, and it no longer was. It was, I suddenly realized with awe, the Past. But what was the Past? And where was it? And now and here, as I lay in bed this winter evening in a New York apartment, listening to my sister playing the piano, Time itself moved on, and tomorrow this dreaming about the past would be the Past, too. It made me feel uneasy. I got no further before I fell asleep.

I thought about it often in the next weeks. Thought is too systematic a word for what I actually did, I am sure. I did not try to solve the problem. I displayed no precocious dialectic virtuosity. I "thought" about it in that I felt about it seriously. I repeatedly had a sense of the dreamlike though intense quality of time past and remembered, the odd unreality of time sure to come but not yet here, the wavering evanescence of the present. Or, as I put it to myself, yesterday is gone; today is going, always going; tomorrow is coming but it *hasn't* come. I used to try to explain it all to people, to the Negro elevator boy, particularly; he seemed to be the only one who would listen, though he said: "You shouldn't worry yo' head about that!" I don't think I found out until five or six years later that I was far from the only one who had been bemused and bepuzzled by the theme. I had a secret feeling that there was something special, private, and abnormal about being worried about such things, just as a child may go on a long time thinking he is the only one bemused and bepuzzled by sex.

But Time was not the only philosophical problem of which I had an early intimation. I was to learn at college, by way of Paulsen's book, of something called the epistemological problem. How do we *know*, and how do we know that we know? I was to learn of metaphysics, the attempt to define scrupulously what was really real. But epistemology and metaphysics came by anticipation into my ken long before I knew the words or the professional arguments about them, or knew that there were grown men who spent their whole lives debating such issues and were paid by universities for doing so and for teaching others how to do it. I cannot lay claim myself to having hit upon the intimations of these things. It was Julian L., now, I am told, a much sought after pediatrist in New York, who was the agent to bring epistemology and metaphysics (though he, too, did not know the words) to my fourteen-year-old attention from out of his fourteen-year-old observation. The fact he pointed at, I discovered much later, is time and again used as a conventional illustration in philosophical treatises.

It was in the mountains on the afternoon of a hot July day. We had been talking drowsily under a tree by the side of a brook. I was almost asleep. Julian was stirring a stick in the water.

"The stick looks broken, doesn't it?" he said.

I looked up vaguely. "Yes; what of it?" I said. I sometimes shared my sister's realism.

"But it isn't; that's only the shadow in the water; it's *unreal*," said Julian. He lapsed into silence, still stirring the stick. "But there's a *real* shadow," he said; "the shadow itself is *real*, all right."

"Yes," I said. "I'm going to sleep for a while."

Julian's remark made little immediate impression. The reality of a shadow, the unreality of a broken stick did not seem to matter very much amid this sunlight on this summer green. But days later, walking by the brook again with Julian and happening to stir a stick in it myself, my friend's comments of the other day suddenly came back with unexpected cogency and vividness into my mind.

"The shadow in a way *is* real," I suddenly said to Julian. Then two fourteen-year-old epistemologists, sitting by a mountain stream, wrestled dialectically, within the limits of their abilities, with the Real and the Unreal, how we knew anything really, and whether seeing was believing. I soon wearied of the controversy—as I have often done since. The whole problem, I somehow felt even then, was artificial, as I now think I have sound reasons for believing it to be. But the theme haunted me, and often that summer I reverted to it. Dreams, too, were like shadows, and the things one remembered were like dreams. I tried, without success even by my own fourteen-year-old standards, to write a poem about it.

Indeed, even now it seems to me that the whole matter is a better theme for poetry than inquiry, and is poetic in its origins and fruits rather than primarily a genuine problem for analysis. The net effect for the time being was to make me a solitary solipsist—how I should have loved the words had I known them!—and I would pretend for as long as I could, till I was too hungry or too tired, that our house, my bed, the meat and milk and eggs at supper, the other summer visitors, Julian himself, were merely shadows or dreams in my mind, and that I myself perhaps was a dream. I seem to remember my mother found me particularly and annoyingly absent-minded the next week or two. It was fun to treat the world round about me as apparitions to my understanding and imagination. Many years later Santayana invented for such dreams, such passing appearances, such momentary objects of intuition, the term "essences." I had not realized until I began to recall these early explorations of epistemology that I had come upon essences long ago.

It was through Julian, too, at the same time, that I first began to think about Freedom and Determinism, Fate and Chance, Necessity and Accident, though, of course, not remotely in those terms. My friend and I used to discuss occasionally the accident that had brought us together in a friendship that, we were certain, would never end. It was a lucky accident, we decided. But the very luck of it, we re-decided, *proved* that it was something more than luck; that it *could* not have been an accident. For look, we unanimously agreed, our parents, who had not known each other, must first have decided to come to the same place and, all un-known to each other, to rent houses directly opposite each other. It was not an accident. It was an inevitable chain; it was *intended*. It was Fate. And it was part of Fate, we warmly agreed, that we should be friends for ever. Fate and Freedom, these are the familiar preoccupations of theologians from St. Paul and St. Augustine down. So are death and immortality. Many philosophical conceptions, I was to learn later, have their origins in the mind of the child and the mind of the savage. There is a whole library about primitive conceptions of the soul. The appearance of dead men in dreams, if I remember, is supposed to lead the primitive warrior to believe that his dead friends and enemies live in another world. I cannot say that I can recall having been concerned very early with the nature of the soul or the problem of immortality. Nor early to have brooded upon death. Death was what happened to *old* people, people in their forties and fifties or seventies; to people's grandparents, not to anybody one really knew or played with. The death of a boy in our group— Herbert, the fat, good-natured, not very literary member of our Benjamin Franklin Club—first gave me pause and led me to think of the quite incredible fact of death. When older people died, it was as if they had simply gone off or moved away. And in any case one had never known them very well, and adults, besides, did strange things. But Herbert, the liveliest of all, simply gone, stretched out in a coffin and carried away and buried! It was far more upsetting than when Mr. S., the father of one of my friends, died. That was sad and sudden. He came home from a trip, had pneumonia; they brought an oxygen tent for him to breathe in, and three days later he was gone. But *he* was bald-headed and had always seemed incredibly old; he was fifty. It seemed odd not to see him emerge at the aristocratically late hour of a quarter to nine and in his top hat leisurely set off for the local rather than the urgent express train on the Elevated. His son, my chum, wore a black tie and mourning-band and was not allowed to go to the theatre and acquired for a while a special dignity and importance. But that was different. The death of one of us, a contemporary, was another matter. The very young believe not in immortal life, but in eternal life here on earth; it struck me as incredible that anyone, any young person, should really die, simply cease to be. And yet I am convinced that one's adult philosophical opinions are formed in embryo very early, if one is going to have them at all. For it never seemed to me that my friend was living as an angel in some other world. He had ceased simply to be. Death was the end, and there both the incredibility and the sadness of it lay. Death, like birth, was a fact of existence, as inevitable and as natural. I vaguely felt that as a child; I definitely think that now.

But the intimations of immortality that Wordsworth speaks of have, of course, nothing to do with an after-life. They have to do with a sense of something "far more deeply interfused," a presence of something permeatingly beautiful in the crass or exquisite surface of things. Like every child I felt, especially, I think, in the art of music, an adumbration of something acute in its poignancy and intensity, yet otherworldly in its distance from ordinary objects. It doesn't matter much that it was nothing more musically profound than "Angel's Serenade" or *Kammenoi Ostrov* or the *Tannhäuser* Bacchanale that gave me this sense, or that it seldom came from anything commonly called real. If it did not come from music, it came from poetry, and the poetry, too, did not have to be too profound.

I think I know now precisely where I received my introduction to mystical and transcendental philosophy, I think it was again the accident of knowing Julian that introduced to me the genre of thought that regards this world as simply the half-veil, half-revelation of a world beyond phenomena. Julian's father was a business man by day, by night one of those philosophers without portfolio whom I have earlier described in this book. In his leisure he played with philosophical ideas. He saw in me a possible initiate. Initiate is a rightly chosen word, for it was to a "secret wisdom" that he introduced me. He proceeded to enlighten me, since he had apparently given his son up as uninterested, concerning theories which I could only vaguely understand, though they seemed to me impressive, and about which to this day I do not think Mr. L. was very clear. I did cloudily gather from him what he had gathered from the purple-bound volumes of a writer whose initials alone appeared upon his work, "T. K." I did not, nor did he, know who the mysterious T. K. was, and never since have I been able to find T. K.'s works in any library. I have since, often enough, encountered ideas not unlike, as I remember them, those of that retiring author, at least as they were mediated to me by my friend's theosophical-minded father. Mr. L. lent me one of T. K.'s books, but I found the words and the sentences too long and too many. The main themes, however, were relatively clear to me as they were transmitted with grave enthusiasm by T. K.'s disciple. The world of matter about us was not the real world. It was the shadow of a world far truer and deeper and more real than that which we meet through the senses. The real (or the divine) world consisted of spiritual beings whose choral dance of Truth and Beauty constituted the order and beauty of our visible world, so far as through virtue or wisdom or genius we could touch them. The important thing for us was to put ourselves in touch with these invisible spiritual beings, with this order of Truth beyond phenomena. Mr. L. used some of these words, and though I did not quite know what they meant (and am not sure I know now), they sounded grand and serious. Only much later did I read the same thing—more or less—but put more clearly and cogently in the writings of Plotinus, the second-century Greek mystic and dialectician. Not until many years later did I realize that the doctrine of T. K. and of Julian's father had its roots in Plato and Plotinus and Augustine and in India's immemorial past.

Some imp or angel of common-sense used to prompt me to argue with T. K.'s prophet. Something in me then warned me, as it articulately does now, to distrust all such high breathlessness in thought. And I made as good a case as I could for the reality of the world of the senses and the distrust of any alleged world beyond it. But even then I was moved, as I am still moved, by the suasion of any such poetic speculations, and I have always been grateful that a business-man amateur interpreting a theosophist should thus early have awakened a feeling in me, a sympathy with "the light that never was on sea or land." I felt then, as I feel now, that the mystics are talking about a world practically "unreal," and spiritually more real than common-sense allows.

Not until I came to college did I find out that philosophy, in the hands of its greatest practitioners, often arose in a search for, often resulted in a programme or a set of prin-ciples of, the Good Life, and that when a philosophy is taken seriously it is or becomes a Moral Philosophy. Morals in our neighbourhood in my childhood, and I suspect in most neighbourhoods of the period, had to do with sex chiefly, and immorality meant just one thing and it was better not to say out loud what that was. I don't think I was ever greatly troubled by the question, "What is the Good?" The good was defined by the standards of one's own family and the families that one knew. Moral philosophy arises historically, one is led to believe, when the conventional codes are collapsing, and rival theories of good and evil, competing standards of value, come in conflict with each other. No rival and competing standards seemed to be clashing in our neighbourhood, though I read now that it was a period of transition. There were the toughs in the tenements only two blocks away, but that was another world.

The only very early social scepticism I can recall developing came from the high school classmate whose family was bitterly poor and who had to work hard and long after school at odd jobs. The neat world of accepted values, the decorous respectability of middle-class life and its economic foundations, all were called into question for me by the fact that this friend of mine had to work after school and that he had to stay in the city in the summer. But it was not only his example; it was his instruction that made me query the operations of right and wrong in the small world I knew. Ben F. was an Austrian immigrant, two or three years older than myself; he seemed to me to look quite grown up. He certainly had read grown-up books. Within a year I was pattering after him a denunciation of the capitalist system, and I accompanied him to Madison Square Garden to cheer, for twenty minutes, Eugene V. Debs. I did not quite know anything about Marx's labour theory of value, but I knew people were underpaid, that the rich exploited the poor, that society must be made over, that there must be equality of opportunity and reward for all. Then, among other things, Ben wouldn't have to work afternoons and could spend his summer vacations in the country, like me, perhaps with me. My economic understanding was primitive enough, and my enthusiasm for social justice as vague as it was enthusiastic. But such as they were, they led me to the portals of moral philosophy. Perhaps, I began to suspect, all that I thought just and proper was itself a middle-class family prejudice. There must be other ways of living, other ways of looking at right and wrong in the world.

I suspect many moral philosophers have begun through being thus accidentally disquieted at about the age of thirteen, and the search for the Good has begun usually because some boy somewhere discovered early that there was something wrong with the *good* people he knew and found people outside his own family who had other standards of good than he had ever dreamed of. But in my own case, the reflection upon the good life had a long intermission and I was not consciously aware that there was such a thing as moral philosophy until long after I had stumbled upon it. Just about this time I discovered poetry, and then I quite forgot the Good Society, and the evils of the one in which I comfortably, and Ben uncomfortably, lived.

It turned out that I was not to think much more about "philosophy" in the strict sense until my freshman year in college. Such general ideas as a high-school pupil gets in America come, I think, largely from literature and history. There is a superstition even among college administrators that philosophy is a subject too "deep" and too "hard" for the underclassman. I picked up (most high-school pupils do) such logic as I got from geometry or outlining Burke's Speech on Conciliation, and such moral philosophy as filtered through in the *Sir Roger de Coverley Papers* and the *Idylls of the King* and the *Rubaiyat of Omar Khayyam*. But as I recall these early intimations of philosophical thought, I wonder why, as in France, philosophy cannot be begun earlier. The themes of reality and unreality, of good and evil, of fate and necessity, of determinism and freedom, the method of thinking itself, the being or the illusion of time are surely themes that early haunt the imagination of all but the most dull among adolescents. Once in the Public Library I browsed among the "100" books, where the inventor of the Dewey decimal system long since elected to place philosophy. The librarian put me off onto *The Three Musketeers* and *Les Misérables*. But I rather wish now that youngsters were brought to philosophy when it naturally springs upon their imaginations. When they come upon it in college it is a subject to be studied. But I am sure many of them, like myself, come upon it much earlier. The stick broken in water, the sense of something deep and far, felt by the sea or in the hills on a summer day, the puzzle and the pathos of time, the uneasiness about the good, have raised questions that one ought not to have to wait until late in one's college career to hear treated as questions worthy of being answered —or of being asked.

NINETEEN

Fashions in Ideas

THE philosopher Alfred North Whitehead has, I believe, made current the phrase "climate of opinion" to describe the intellectual atmosphere in which people in a given period live. As I look back on what I hope is not more than half a lifetime spent mostly in New York, I become conscious of how much ideas are transmitted by a kind of osmosis, like those tricks of manner and even of voice that two people, long married, are said to catch from each other. Once long ago I had lunch with the editor of a monthly magazine, then distinguished, or just ceasing to be so. The editor was a bright, youngish man, too busy lecturing all around the country (and in the intervals editing his magazine and writing monthly homiletics for it) to read or to think. He made it a practice, he told me, to get his education at lunch. His teachers consisted of the people he talked to over the luncheon table in any given week, and, judging by the list he recited, he was shrewd in his choice of luncheon tutors. Nor was he a fool about picking up the essence of things whose details or whose foundations he would never have had the time, the industry, or the inclination to study, or to understand. Over the coffee once I recall giving him by request a *précis,* altogether sketchy, of Dewey's philosophy of education. He made quite a good article out of it, and showed the weak points of progressive education and experimental philosophy quite as well as if he had taken the trouble to understand their strong ones.

I was a little contemptuous of the method, and I am so still. But we all get our education partly at lunch or dinner. Certainly in New York the "climate of opinion" is compounded of the things that are said in the book reviews, and at the dinner tables and in the after-dinner conversation of those who live in the market-place or among the suburbs of ideas. For the fact is that ideas among the talking literate have become a sublimated gossip. For a month or for a season, an idea or a theory spreads like a rumour or a scandal over the intelligentsia of New York. Soon it races, like a pulse or a song, over the whole country. One year it is the theory of the leisure class, another year technocracy; a season passes and it is abstractionism in painting, logical positivism in philosophy, Anglo-Catholicism (or Anglo-Communism) in religion, the folklore of capitalism, or relativity in physics. Ideas painfully thought out in the study or worked out in the laboratory, or sometimes tossed off the top of some facile mind with a quick insight and a gift for phrase, become thinned down into the chit-chat of the salons. Einstein works years over his mathematical formulas and on a sudden relativity becomes the gossip of the clubs, the studies, and the dinner tables. A sociological study might be made of the time lag between the discovery of ideas and their popular or their snob appeal. Along with my contemporaries I have lived through many fashions in ideas: Dewey, Bergson, Freud, Marx, Einstein, T. S. Eliot, Liberalism, Progressive Education, Fascism, Communism, Neo-Thomism, Progress, Disillusion, Reform, Revolution. By the time this book will have appeared, there will, I am sure, be some new ism to have taken possession of the articulates.

When one is very young, the first fashion in ideas that one meets does not seem in the least to be simply a fashion. It seems most likely the sudden revelation of an eternal truth. For, after all, how should one know, meeting one's first vogue for the first time, that it is a vogue? It is natural enough to mistake an epidemic for a norm; born during a whirlwind, one might think it the ordinary weather of the world.

In the years just before America entered the World War, Liberalism (which I am told is, but do not believe to be, dead) was the current fashion. How was a young man at college to know that Liberalism had some of the marks of a dying cause? It was in its origins the expression of a hopeful and expanding democratic and capitalistic world; it had its roots in a nineteenth-century England that itself was rapidly being transformed. The language and the hopes of the laboratory (as Joseph Wood Krutch pointed out in *The Modern Temper*) were being carried over to revive the hopes and certainly to stud the conversation of mankind, at least of the intellectuals in New York. Of course a good deal of mankind elsewhere was being slaughtered in large quantities by the discoveries of the laboratory. But that was, we believed, only a temporary setback, and we hoped optimistically that cooperative aspiration, engineered by intelligence, would give us a brave new world—a phrase which would not at the time, I think, have been used ironically. Walter Lippmann,

after assisting Santayana at Harvard and being secretary to
the Socialist Mayor of Schenectady, had written a gallant
summons in *Preface to Politics*. He and all of us learned a lot
from his teacher, Graham Wallas, who showed the workings
of *Human Nature in Politics* and wrote another book on *The
Art of Thought*. "Social psychology" had just about been
discovered, and "behaviourism," too. H. G. Wells was pam-
pering our hopes with the *Research Magnificent,* the image of
a "House of Solomon" that was to remake mankind. The
New Republic was founded, and in good prose on clear paper
made weekly blueprints of a rational future. After a hundred
weeks, as somebody remarked, it seemed a hundred years
old. John Dewey had invented, and many mouthed as a
slogan, "intelligent control"; James Harvey Robinson was
pleading for the adult mind in place of the savage and child
mind in the direction of human affairs; we must not have a
sixteenth-century tradesman's mentality to control the twen-
tieth-century motorcar that was modern civilization. Though
it dated from an earlier time, Swinburne's line from his
"Hymn to Man" might well have been the signature of the
talk of the minds of the town: "Glory to man in the highest,
for man is the master of things."

Even the pulpit was infected by the latter-day salvation-
ism. Theology itself became a gospel of social reform. There
was endless talk of Liberalism and the Churches, and the
Liberalism alluded to was touched with scientific hopes.

No one knows how long that fashion would have lasted
had not the war intervened (though there is no great reason
for believing that as a fashion it would have lasted more than
any other). When ideas are used primarily as subjects of
conversation, the subjects grow wearisome and new ones

must be found. It was a shock to me to discover that this
first climate of opinion I had ever known was temporary,
almost as much a shock as the first time a young contemporary of my schooldays had died. One would not have thought
that either would or could vanish. And like the memory of
those whom one has known well and who have died young,
those early imbibed ideas remain as controlling images. It is
hard for me; it is hard, I suspect, for anyone who grew up
during the fashion of pre-war scientific hopes and liberal
enthusiasms to believe that that vocabulary is quite out-
moded or that the hopes which it expressed are dead. There
are certainly good reasons for questioning that language, the
naïve transference of the words of the physical laboratory to
the passions and conflicts of men. There are reasons, patent
in every news dispatch from China, Spain, or Central Europe, for doubting whether those pre-war hopes, rosy and
seductively clear, were ever well founded. But whether or
not there is any longer any ground for the hope of making
through intelligence and goodwill a brand-new, brave new
world, the chatter in the salons is certainly different now.
One reads a different language in the intellectual weeklies,
and even in some of the authors—those of them who are
still alive and active—among whom I was brought up.
Some of these latter, like H. G. Wells, indeed still use the
same language. It seems a pallid echo; nobody listens to it
and nobody babbles it after dinner any more.

The first change I observed was right after the war, the
period of disillusion. That has been discussed time and again,
and its most reasoned and complete statement came in Joseph Wood Krutch's *The Modern Temper*. But the history of
that book itself reflects the difference between *ideas* and the

climate of ideas. The title, *The Modern Temper,* is, I suppose, familiar to thousands. For a season, as was said later of technocracy, one would have had to walk into a sound-proof room not to hear the name mentioned. Yet the book had a relatively small actual circulation and not many of those who swore by it as their negative creed of disillusion (though its theme was really rational scepticism) had the industry to read as well as talk about it. They read the reviews, or heard quotations from the reviews. A whole spate of writers, Aldous Huxley notably, in his pre-Buddhist days, fed the cult of spiritual weariness or contempt or revulsion.

For one of the ways in which ideas become fashionable is not through reasoned analysis, but through their being broached in novels and plays. Ideas, just beginning to fade in the seminars, appear, watered down, in the novels in the circulating libraries. Or they appear behind the footlights to people in evening dress who come as late to ideas as they come to the theatre, as late, often, as the dramatists themselves. The ideas that found their tardy way into novels and plays constituted what Frederick Lewis Allen has called "The Credo of the Highbrows."

Religion and romantic love were both illusions; American life was dull and standardized; the liberal hopes had been rendered fantastic and foolish by the chaos of the post-war world; life could at best offer ironic gaiety and beauty, itself not to be taken too seriously. There was, it will be remembered, much talk about flaming youth, but nobody talked much about a hard, gem-like flame. One heard rather, from Edna St. Vincent Millay, about burning candles at both ends. The light was admitted to be lovely, but it would not last the night.

Meanwhile one had been hearing increasingly about Freud. Again it took me (it took many, I am sure) some little time to distinguish between the ideas themselves and their fashionable currency. It is hard to say how much good ideas have suffered from their modishness and been impeded by their very popularity. There is, I suppose, no serious writer on human affairs who would withhold tribute to the fundamental depths and importance of the psycho-analytic contribution to the understanding of human motives. Hardly any well-informed person (though there are a few) would contest the immense therapeutic value psycho-analytic treatment has afforded in vast numbers of cases. But the depths of the ideas and their great curative possibilities are not what I mean by psycho-analysis as a fashion. I mean the days, somewhat over now, when a smattering of psycho-analytic terms studded all conversation everywhere, and even the gossip about friends and enemies had to take a psycho-analytic turn. One knew or one suspected everybody's complexes. Where, earlier, people would have spoken of brashness and rudeness, they spoke now of compensation and an inferiority complex. One's friends were no longer unhappy, but frustrated; castles in Spain gave place to wish fulfilments, and no weekend was complete without an amateur psycho-analytic devastation of everybody not present and in turn of everybody there.

It is not easy to say just when it was that the vocabulary of the dinner parties and the little groups began to change. Some say it came with the depression; I seem to remember noticing it a little earlier. But suddenly it seemed (however gradual it may have been) the talk had turned from sex to socialism. There was even a revival, for a brief, frenzied period, of the ideal of a civilization run by science, this time through the engineers. Technocracy was the name of that short-lived epidemic. It seems incredible now that for months that word to describe a civilization to be saved through engineers and engineering (despite the failure of Herbert Hoover) was the magic symbol, the shibboleth, that dominated the conversation of the intellectuals. There was a flood of books and pamphlets, formulas and statistics; whole forests must have been destroyed to provide the printed matter that nourished the fad. And in a few months the whole forest of printed matter disappeared, and technocracy was as dead as Queen Victoria.

This is not a chapter of history but of reminiscence, and I cannot say I remember exactly when Marxism first became, pro and con, a staple part of the fashionable diet of ideas. Certainly Marxism to the literate was not new; had we not been required in 1914 to read the *Communist Manifesto* as part of our reading in a regulation, though exceptionally good, course in European history? But books on art and metaphysics and novels and plays were not then discussed in terms of their Rightness or Leftness; one heard little about the Party Line, and Dialectic Materialism was unknown to most hostesses, even as a label. The world was not divided so definitely into Left and Right that anyone would have been prompted to write, or be scolded by certain correspondents for writing, the following verses which I published in the *Nation* some years ago:

> *Left meant left when I was a lad,*
> *And Right meant right—not simply bad;*
> *These terms, both simple and geographic,*

And principally used in directing traffic,
Were each of them spelt with a quite small letter.
Not even the teachers knew any better.
Now each has become a Moral Sign,
Dividing the race by a bitter line,
So that each of us knows who is good and bad,
Which none of us knew when I was a lad.

And the same holds true of Red and White,
Once the names for lovely forms of light,
The red of lips, or of skies at dawn,
Or geraniums glowing near a deep green lawn.
And I sigh for the days when left meant left
And weep in a world of peace bereft,
For the days when red meant a summer rose,
And white meant a mountain clad in starlit snows.

I am not speaking of serious students of Marxism, nor of the importance of the Marxian understanding of history and politics. I am speaking again of the fact that at a certain point in the history of conversation among the articulates of New York, Marxism became the characteristic theme of conversation and almost a correct standard of intellectual deportment. It cannot be attributed to the Russian Revolution, for the Revolution had taken place in 1917 and between 1917 and 1929 there were many other fashions of ideas.

But it was some time before Marxism could be the comprehensive atmosphere in which all conversation was bathed. Even today while the strategy of revolution is being discussed in one corner, and there are vivid debates as to how likely it is that the possessing classes will consent to be expropriated without violence, other choruses are sung in other corners. For a time it was relativity, although there was general agreement that nobody (save a dozen men whose names nobody remembered) could understand Einstein. That agreement, however, in which most discussions began, was no bar to talking about the Einstein theory, or even making diagrams of two trains moving at different speeds to illustrate how relative time was. Then there was the winter that Eddington's *Nature of the Physical World* was published, and Sir James Jeans revealed the philosophical mysteries of *The Mysterious Universe*. It is hard to remember now the easy way conversationists had with the principle of indetermination, time-space, and quanta. If any one suggested that Jeans and Eddington were superimposing some very questionable —and old-fashioned—metaphysics upon their scientific researches, that Eddington remained fundamentally a Quaker who happened to be playing with quanta, such reservations were for one short winter not the mode.

In still another corner would be a young man who had discovered St. Thomas Aquinas, seven hundred years late, and found in the clear principles of that orthodox summit of Catholic orthodoxy the one way of life for a rational animal, and a most impressive vocabulary. Behaviourism and psycho-analysis had run their course, and it was years since anybody (save economic scholars) had mentioned Veblen, whose *Theory of the Leisure Class* and whose phrase "conspicuous waste" had once been in all literate mouths. Watson, the founder of behaviourism, had been forgotten and was now in the advertising business, and Bergson, whose lectures in French were attended by Frenchless fashionable ladies, was (most people believed) dead. Meanwhile, the free association prose, the introspective streams of consciousness of Proust and Virginia Woolf, began to be more than audible murmurs, "the cult of unintelligibility" began in poetry, and the breakdown of all familiar conventions in surrealist painting. In that time it was bliss to be alive, and to be young was heaven, a heaven filled with singular stars and strange colours, some of them resuscitated, like Aquinas, from a half-forgotten past, as if somebody should declare after looking at the pictures in the Pitti Palace in Florence that he had found the secret of Raphael's blue, or that the methods of the Primitives were the only techniques for modern painting to follow.

It is natural, living in New York, and moving among acquaintances generated by the writing and teaching profession, that I should have been exposed in succession to all these modes. I discovered, furthermore, when one left New York one heard the same things, usually, that one had heard in Manhattan the previous winter, in transformed farmhouses in Connecticut, in cafés in Paris, on transatlantic steamers. What, I began to wonder, accounts for these changes in fashions of ideas, so much more rapid in their succession among us than they are abroad? What is there that has made many of these discussions so superficial that the term "intellectual," from being a term naturally enough taken to imply praise as an adjective, has come to have the atmosphere of contempt about it as a noun. I suspect one of the answers lies in the fact that the intellectuals are more interested in articulateness than in analysis, and in themes for conversation than in objects for feeling and thought. The parlour pink, the salon scientist, the drawing-room philosopher, the tea-time psychologist or theologian, are not new in our era. They were rampant in France in the eighteenth century. But the polite world of learning was then a smaller world, and though it is still small (the class of intellectuals is never as large as its fluency would lead one to expect), it had then none of the devices of high-pressure publicity that can rapidly make it as obligatory to have a certain vocabulary as to wear certain kinds of clothes. A clever publisher can make even the austere history of philosophy a story that everyone must know or read or claim to have read.

There is nothing heinous about the love of words for their own sake. Was it not Plato himself who said that he would never write a treatise on philosophy, that the latter must be acquired by conversation, the flame leaping from speaker to speaker "until the soul itself caught fire"? "Education at lunch" may be a poor affair, but everyone knows how out of a conversation new insights emerge and one's old ones become clarified. But what one could see time and again in New York was the love of words in the place of ideas, and, even worse, simply the love of knowing and displaying the words, clichés cherished for their snob values, or new and current generalizations paraded like the latest fashions in ties or hats. Even noble words standing for noble causes have in our time come to be debased into such clichés. Anti-war and anti-Fascism can become mere labels and signals, and by the same token so can Democracy and Socialism. The *Tyranny of Words* has itself, to borrow Mr. Stuart Chase's stereotype, become a "stereotype," and the *Folklore of Capitalism* itself a fashionable mythology.

Impatience with the talking intellectuals may thus easily bring the whole intellectual life into disrepute. I have heard talking fools dismiss the talkers time and again. It is easy

enough for the stupid or the dull or the reactionary to mistake intellectual gossip for the intellectual life, and argue
from the chatter, polysyllabic but trivial, of the salons that
the intellect itself is to be condemned. Our current conserva-
tives are not the first to identify all thinking with sophistry.
Socrates himself was put to death partly because he was
thought to be one of the glibly talking Sophists who had
come to Athens and that, like them, he was teaching young
Athenians to talk without knowing what they were talking
about—which was what Socrates convicted all Athens of doing. But the respectable suspicion of Socrates was plausible,
for Socrates himself had become a fashion with the young
wits of Athens. The dull and the conservative know only
that there is a lot of talk going on, that it is dull to them,
that what chiefly recommends ideas (to those whose
intellectual life is nearly all talk) is that they are new and
that they can be talked about. To the man without a gift for
conversation, or the passion for it, all conversation must
seem so much chatter and not least so the conversation of
the intellectuals. The intellectuals themselves have sometimes
felt this about themselves. Every once in a while in New
York, at some crowded cocktail party or at some dinner
party of the well-fed, the well-clothed, and the well-
informed, one hears the desire, usually well expressed, to get
away from all the talk. The "*faux-naïf*" itself becomes a fashion, and the silences and the simplicities become the theme
of talk, and everyone moves to the country to continue the
talk there in a barn made into a studio.

Yet the conservative and the dull are mistaken if they
think the chatter that has been current in New York in the
last two decades is unimportant. I suspect that the real grudge

of the reactionary (rather than the dull) against the articulates is their shrewd perception that the chatter is symptomatic. They realize (what is true) that some of the modes of intellectual life which have become fashionable are symptoms of a deeper uneasiness (shared sometimes by themselves) and of a nervous search for values in place of those no longer adequate. Psycho-analysis may have become a theme for dinner-table conversation and a luxury for moneyed and leisured neurotics. But it never would have taken hold, its favourite terms would never have found their way almost into common speech, unless there had been a recognition of something fresh and important in them. Fascism and Communism are words to bandy about; one may sometimes, in New York, think they are *boutonnières* rather than banners. One may long to be among Vermont farmers who have scarcely heard of them (though one may be sure that the summer residents will have done so). But Fascism and Communism are not less serious because they, in certain mouths, become chit-chat. They are symptoms of new forces in the world; they are patterns of life, of which the chatter in the salons is merely (but none the less really) symptomatic.

There is any amount of loose talk about tight and subtle doctrines, which are in their own right of the greatest importance: Neo-Thomism over the cocktails, surrealism over the cigarettes, relativity while floating on a rubber mattress in a mountain pool on an August weekend! Like everybody else interested in words and ideas, I have participated in such goings-on. But let it be remembered that while leisured men and women in the eighteenth century were talking in the salons or the formal gardens, they were but the babbling surface of a deeper ferment. I think that is what the anti-intellectuals suspect and fear. It is not the intellectuals they are inveighing against, or loose talk, or the passion for novelty, or the forgetfulness of old important ideas, or the lack of discipline or exactness or responsibility in so much that passes for intellectual conversation. They would not, I think, mind these things so much, for such faults they share and can sympathize with. But the anti-intellectual prejudice is a prejudice against genuine intellection, actual thought. The anti-intellectuals know, correctly, that if the talk goes on long enough, new and disquieting ideas may get about, and the security of the world they know, and have a private interest in preserving, may be destroyed—for the illusions by which it is maintained will be punctured. There would be even more prejudice against real thinking than against conversational play with ideas; the anti-intellectualism of every reactionary regime in Europe illustrates the point.

One can be amused or bored by the talkers, but, as the entrenched and the smug know, *thinking* is cause for alarm. One can smile at the Sophists but nothing less than execution will do for Socrates. The entrenched know also that what started as a fashion may turn out to be a creed or a system of life or of politics. Christianity for a time seemed a harmless vogue among the more socially exalted ladies of Rome, and ideas are dangerous when they become endeared to the rich and the polite.

But there is one set of talkers I have heard who in the long run may be even more important than are the snobs. Isms and ideologies are the special delight of the brighter young in the universities, who ape the language that is current among their writing and talking elders. The current fashions in thought and talk must seem to some of them—I know they *do* seem to some of them—eternal truths. Older people, especially those who have never stopped being spiritual adolescents themselves, are inclined to smile at the young intellectuals. But some among these young men with special energy, imagination, and zeal, will one day take seriously some of the doctrines they talk about as programmes for action, not merely as topics for discussion. Karl Marx and Mussolini were both young intellectuals once. Fashions in ideas, especially among the young, are barometers—though it is, alas, impossible to tell which barometer is which. Many "young intellectuals" will simply graduate into the adult salons and continue talking the remainder of their lives, catching each new craze or mumbling, as slippered pantaloons, the ones they first caught at college. But one or another among them will have been touched to flame by a formula, and have the power to communicate the flame. The talk in the college commons, I have long suspected, may be more portentous than the discussions at the Faculty Club. These fledgelings, for one thing, have a longer life before them, and some of them will have time and energy to turn the word into flesh. Some idea just coming into fashion may be more than a fashion or an idea before they get through with it, and the babble of some current undergraduate may some day mature into the inspiration by which the world is moved.

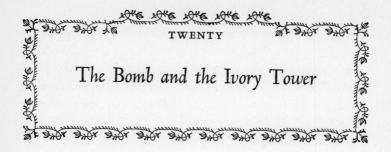

TWENTY

The Bomb and the Ivory Tower

THE title of my closing chapter is, I confess, melodramatic. This book, though it has touched on principles, has dealt with them mostly as they arose from incidents in my memory. Now I have not known bombs at first hand, have witnessed no wars, been privy to no revolutions. Nor can a university whose very stationery reminds one that it is in the City of New York be described as an Ivory Tower. There are no dreaming spires at Columbia, nor stately pleasure domes, nor is it easy to attain æsthetic or philosophic detachment in a place of higher learning that has contributed brain trusts to help the government and edify the humorists, that maintains a school of journalism, and that has a school of philosophy which, under the inspiration of John Dewey, holds philosophy itself to have social origins and social consequences. But there are, even at urban universities in the twentieth century, liberated spirits to be met; the free mind can keep its quiet even among the noises and alarums. For all the horrible news on the front page each day and all the noisy distractions, one can be as detached in New York as in any village, and though one may be at one of the cross-roads of civilization, one is after all remote from an actual military front. I once *heard* of a bomb being thrown near where I was. It was in Florence during the first year of the Fascist domination of Italy. Some elderly ladies had been told by someone who had been told by someone that a bomb had been thrown in the Piazza San Miniato. It was the talk of the *pensione* the whole evening. But the rumour turned out to be false.

The "The Bomb and the Ivory Tower" is intended, of course, symbolically. Ever since I can remember thinking and feeling about the world at all, I have been torn between the conception of the world all threats, alarms, and obligations, and the vision of it as an arcanum of delighted perception, a spectacle to be enjoyed, endured, and understood. The Bomb and the Ivory Tower seem to me as good symbols as any. Ever since adolescence I have realized how the bombs of the actual tormented contemporary scene break in upon the Ivory Tower of appreciation and understanding. The bombs are real enough now, in all conscience, though they be in China and Spain. But less literal though no less devastating bombs break in upon us daily, and it is not even inconceivable that if the steel ones break out all over Europe, despite our disillusion with the last crusade for democracy, they too will again play a part in our national life.

Nobody living in New York and earning his living, even if it be by studying and teaching philosophy, can remain quite in the Ivory Tower. But I have lived in it for periods and by aspiration until I have begun to share the general suspicion into which the ideal has fallen.

I have certainly known the phrase, in its metaphorical

sense, almost as long as I can remember. I had heard it used so long as the name for æsthetic exquisiteness and romantic disillusioned flight from the world of action and of mediocrity that I had never realized until a year or two ago that I had not the slightest idea where the label came from. I found it by accident one day, through the characteristic febrile enterprise of *Time*. That publication for some reason (I think in connexion with a review of Santayana's novel) wished to find out where the phrase originated, and lighted upon me, via the telephone, to find out. I take it a professor of philosophy seemed a likely enough person to know. I did not know, nor did my colleagues whose specialties were English, French, or philosophy. Nearly everybody thought Walter Pater was responsible, or possibly some of the French Symbolist poets. Finally somebody was persistent enough to discover the source. The metaphor was given currency in its familiar metaphorical sense by Sainte-Beuve's comments on a poem of Lamartine's called "*La Tour d'Ivoire.*"

But if I did not know the origin of the phrase, I very well recall the emergence of the feeling which it is used to express. Every sensitive high-school boy, I dare say, has known it, the first half-pleasurable, half-painful discovery that there is an enclosure of exquisite things in which one may find refuge from the realm of banality or hardness or futility or brutality which encompasses him—or which perhaps he unendurably feels to encompass him. For me, as for many, poetry and music were the first realms of gold in which I discovered the goodly states and countries of the mind and senses and spirit. The world closes in upon us in our infancy; it oppresses us in our adolescence. And then comes the delicious discovery of "a world elsewhere" in which one can live. The high school

with its stale routine and stale smells, the curriculum with its
hateful algebra and its regimented classes, was still there. The
starched collars in which the children of my generation were
imprisoned was still there. But there was "the immemorial
murmur of innumerable bees" in poetry, and the heard
melodies of music. There were a few friends to walk with
along the beach, and with whom one exchanged misquota-
tions in the moonlight. "All I know of a certain star," one of
them would begin, and another continue, "Is that its light will
travel far." Or one found the *Rubaiyat* and murmured with
sweet sadness about "A book of verses underneath the bough,
a jug of wine, a loaf of bread—and thou beside me singing in
the wilderness," or thought of the days when one would be
gone, and they would turn down an empty glass. A recent
autobiographer has written at the age of thirty-seven a long
book about himself, showing how his romantic young spirit
was turned to reality by immersion in the revolutionary
movement. Even after the Revolution, I suspect, there will
be youngsters of fifteen and sixteen finding their Ivory Tower
in poetry and music, though there will not be any longer any
middle class with its bridge-playing (whist it was in my boy-
hood) and stuffiness to feel superior to in one's exquisite alti-
tude. I was only one among a lot of little Matthew Arnolds
scorning Philistia,

> *While we who are of purer fire,*
> *Emulate the starry choir.*

But even at that early age the bombs begin bursting about
the adolescent spirit. Mine came in the form of the discovery
of economic injustice, as typified by my classmate Ben,
whose father was a janitor, who loved poetry just as much

as I did but who had to spend long afternoons and Sundays minding a telephone switchboard. Bombs came, too, by way of the discourse of a socialist uncle who had come from Germany with fixed ideas that they ordered these things both more efficiently and more equitably there. The middle-class world may have been stuffy but it at least provided comfort, and my musings on poetry and music were interrupted by these early intimations of social injustice and glimpses of a co-operative commonwealth that would make many people less forlorn.

At college I recall being one of many who were torn between lyricism and Liberalism. The Liberalism, for the more literary, amounted chiefly to the feeling that through co-operative intelligence society could be made over so that *everybody* could go to the Philharmonic on Friday afternoons and have pocket editions of the *Shropshire Lad*. By the end of my college days, I had come so completely under the spell of John Dewey and Deweyism that I, for one, felt that even the Philharmonic and Housman must wait; the important thing was to devise a method, through organized intelligence, for making the world over. A New Puritanism had descended on many of us. We felt that the goods of life must be postponed until the world had been made better. When America entered the war, it must be confessed, we were given both pause and perplexity. Slaughter had not been included among the instruments by which creative intelligence was to remake nature and life. But the war seemed to be the necessary preliminary crusade to establish the rule of Democracy and Education in the Western World.

For most educated Americans, at least in the days just after the war, a first trip to Europe was really an escape into an Ivory Tower. Before the war, one gathered, Henry James had fled from the crassness and persistent pioneering crudeness of American life. Just after the war, in similar mood, many young Americans fled from the new standardization, from the backwash of disappointed liberal hopes, and from the oppression by bourgeois aspirations, typified by gadgets and by country clubs. The *précieux,* however, were not the only ones who went to Europe. Philistia went too, on the same steamers. But the Philistines were left to gape at the grim echo of horror in the devastated regions or to go to the Folies Bergère. We who thought of ourselves as burning with purer fire found our ways to the churches and galleries and museums, to the towers of Oxford, the amenities of the sidewalk cafés, especially those with literary associations; to gaze, in a decaying modernity quite unmindful of its decay, at the ruins of a dead Roman civilization whose solemn grandeur is still apparent in the arches of the Pont du Gard near Nîmes; to listen enraptured to the music of Racine as spoken at the Comédie Française, or the harmonies of Mozart at Munich; to be absorbed in the nuances of French food or French speech. We came to look in short even on the living world of Europe with something of the æsthetic traveller's eyes with which we viewed its past. One gathered vaguely from the newspapers on the Continent that there were ominous matters afoot: reparations and disarmament and restless, bitter minorities, and armies of occupation and starved populations in Russia and Germany. But somehow, to one bemused young American at least, these things at the time seemed more unreal than the beautiful surface of the past by which one's eyes and imagination were enriched. Oc-

casionally one had a twinge. Just the day before going to hear
Wagner at the Festspielhaus in Munich, in the autumn of
1920, I visited some elderly ladies to whom I had a letter of
introduction from my distinguished former teacher, Professor Wendell T. Bush—who had lodged with them in his
youth. The exchange rate was giving me, as it was giving all
foreigners, fantastically low prices. These elderly ladies had
hardly enough, on a tiny income, to buy bread and butter;
the bread they could buy was atrocious, butter almost unob-
tainable. They were sweet and kindly and filled with an almost religious veneration of German culture. I must go home
early, they urged, to repose myself for the spiritual strain of
Tristan next day. But they were grateful for the ham their
old friend had asked me to bring them, and quietly full of
hate at the settlement of the war. I talked with embittered
and hopeless Germans in the train and saw pale, obviously
undernourished children in the streets. One heard everywhere bitterness about the Versailles Treaty.

But Reinhardt's Deutsches Theater was superb; Alexander
Moissi made a most tragic and melodious German Hamlet. I
felt I ought not to have had the Royal Box to myself almost
for nothing in an almost empty theatre in Weimar, but the
performance of the *Rosenkavalier* was first rate, and the
cascading and glistening loveliness of its arias and orchestration were, like so many other things in Europe, new to me.
Nürnberg was a boy's dream of medievalism come true,
and Vienna, for all its obvious hunger and raggedness, still
then, as it will perhaps never be again, irresponsible, charming, and gay. What did Dawes plans, Young plans, reparations, matter? Or a possible general strike in England? All
these things, since I had few personal contacts in Europe,

seemed less real or less impinging than the sights and sounds and imaginative loveliness around me. I lived a whole winter through the beginnings of the Fascist regime in Florence. I did not actually see what was happening, or understand very much what it was or portended.

It was a Platonized and an abstracted Europe, a Continent of images that one came to. Even, or perhaps especially, when one read forecasts of the end of European civilization, there seemed all the more reason to treasure the images of its past and be absorbed by them while one could. As I look back on it now, I wonder at my own blindness, except that there were beautiful colours in the lights by which I was dazzled. Nor was I the only one. I say to myself that no intelligent young American could travel that way in Europe now. Europe has ceased to be a picture-book; it has turned into a calendar of portents and alarms. The young traveller, even one in whose head is mostly art history, cannot help, I had thought, feeling these days the tensions of the living and dangerous scene. Most of them do feel them. There are El Grecos still in Spain, but they are stored away now against the risk of bombs, and young Americans, if they go to Spain, go now to fight for the Loyalist cause, not to see El Grecos in the Prado at Madrid, or, as in the past, to gaze upon Toledo in an only apparently slumbering Iberia. Love of the Primitives and of Dante may still bring them to Florence, but they will not be able to avoid seeing and thinking about the less genial Italy of the present. Propaganda leaflets will be placed in their hands; they will see the troops of black-shirted young boys, symptoms innocent but none the less pernicious, of the Italy which now houses the debris of liberty among its more attractive ruins.

The Æsthetic Traveller, I had thought, was dead. But is he? Only this past winter I met several youthful visitors to Italy who hardly knew there was a government, much less an imperialistic and despotic one, and who during the height of the Austrian crisis knew only that there was an obscure Bellini in an obscure church in Venice, and that the Piero della Francesca in the church at San Sepolcro was easier to get to now by bus. When they thought of Vienna, it was of the Vienna Philharmonic, so soon to be ruined, and of the Greek vases, the best in Europe, in the museum there. The Ivory Tower is not quite collapsed, and with a letter of credit in one's pocket and a course in the history of art in one's head, one can still inhabit it for a time in Europe. I still have a lingering sympathy with those who do thus inhabit it. The vistas which hypnotize the young traveller are inno-cent enough, the best residue of civilizations that in their turn, too, were full of cruelty and barbarism. The images of Europe that come from an attempt at understanding its pres-ent are certainly less bewitching, however more enlighten-ing and timely. For a moment or for a season to have lived in imagination among the beautiful documents of a vanished world is wholesome enough. The disease comes from contin-uing to live among them, from mistaking beauties that are the deposit of the past for guides to a future, or from employing them as opiates to avoid thinking about that future. There is much to be said for living among the funded beauties of the great dead as a delight and a refreshment. All action when it is past lives only as an image in the present, as a memory. The cultivated traveller lives in imaginative history, itself simply a longer racial memory. All the troubled present, once it is over, becomes an image recalled, an essence recaptured, sometimes through the help of art. But action is geared to the future, not the past, and it is not to the collections of images in galleries, or to traditions documented in churches or preserved in mellow customs that the traveller in Europe, or the sojourner at home, can turn. Europe to a contemporary understanding is a battleground of more than armies; it is an Armageddon of ideas, and ideas that cut so deeply into the possibilities of the future that one must read them for their portent, not only for their horror. Even without hysteria, in the presence of such portents one must take sides.

Some have tried to live in the Ivory Tower at home. It is less expensive than going to Europe, and soon, indeed, any Ivory Towers to be built will have to be built at home, since there may be no Europe to go to. The returning traveller or the traveller like Thoreau (who said he had travelled much in Concord) has tried to seek an Ivory Tower at home. For life at home, too, even when one is involved in it, may be treated as images, and the sting and venom of it, its pressure and urgency, are half though only half removed. The half-guilty passion of the Æsthetic Traveller in Europe reveals the general plight of the educated man. The images of the art-loving wanderer are largely drawn from the past; he is browsing in his patrimony and responding to inherited beauties. The æsthetic impulses are, I suspect, largely conservative, and that for several reasons. "Our notions of beauty come from our first masters and our first loves," and beautiful forms are, for most people, those forms to which they are exposed very early. Many who are Liberal or Left in their sympathies (because they know we have inherited many outworn cruelties and stupidites along with deathless beauties from the past) are none the less conservative in their imaginative hearts. How many ardent revolutionaries one remembers to have seen at performances of Bach's *B Minor Mass* or the *St. Matthew Passion,* though surely they should be dead set against an art so traditional in its forms and with so much of the religion of the bourgeois in the sources of its inspiration. But if one turns for imaginative nourishment to the past, it is not there one turns for hope. The past that nurtured æsthetic good has left a heritage of war and poverty and injustice that provoke to rebellion and reconstruction precisely those who love the best in the Western tradition. The Æsthetic Traveller ceases dreaming in a past and dreams instead of a future. One hears a good deal of impatient comment on escape to yesterday; it has not been remarked that a vision of tomorrow may also be an "escape." Utopianism is one form of Ivory Tower, no matter how scientific or dialectical the language of its blueprints for human happiness.

There are some who have discovered that in both instances the real bondage is to time, and have sought to escape from the past and the future, from time altogether, into the eternal. There are roughly two ways of escaping from time: one by a rapturous absorption in the moment, one by absorption in things that transcend time altogether. Ecstatic oblivion in the passing moment is an old story historically. The doctrine of it, though doubtless not the practice, began with Epicurus. Though for the moment the doctrine is regarded as either callous or adolescent, it is still practised. It is now called the Importance of Living, and shows signs of becoming fashionable again. In the twenties that doctrine was illustrated in novels about flaming youth and sad young men who had a good time, or, in the moments when they were not having a good time, enjoying themselves proving that life held nothing but the passing moment and that that moment itself held nothing. Rupert Brooke flung himself upon a windy hill, Edna St. Vincent Millay burned her candle at both ends, the sad young heroes and heroines of Scott Fitzgerald flamed—and flickered—in *de luxe* surroundings, and there was a whole section of a whole generation of young and older people who tried to, or alleged they tried to, imitate them. The ideal was the intense moment in a futile world, and among the moments canonized as both most intense and most futile were sex and alcohol. William James once remarked that sex and alcohol, like religion, promoted the *yea-saying* function in man. In the sophisticates of the twenties, at least as one listened to them, these stimulants were valued because they promoted at once the Yea of ecstasy and the Nay of disillusion.

One met in that period, as one still does, those who tried to escape from time not by ignoring the past and the future and concentrating only on today or tonight, but by escaping from time altogether into the eternal, by finding an escape into things that do not change. The flight to the changeless has a long philosophical history, and those who flee to it today likewise call themselves philosophers, though they are often merely playboys, whose playthings are ideas. The mere mention of the theme prompts me to review its origins and to call me back from a philosopher's holiday to a philosopher's business. It would be fun to tell how Heraclitus was both perplexed and edified by the discovery that all is changing under our very eyes and in our very persons themselves. More to the point would be a description of Plato's finding peace and reality in things that did not change, the realm of ideas, the immutable forms of Beauty, Goodness, and Truth.

But that is another story; it is the story of philosophy itself. Here I wish only to remind the reader and myself that there are Platonists without benefit of Plato and many people who, like their (to them, unheard of) predecessor, seek to find escape from time into the eternal. I have seen them discover the eternal in many ways. Sometimes it is in mathematics, or in music. It does not matter when one hears a Bach fugue; it is as if it had been there always; it will always be; it eternally is. There are young men, and older ones, who, sad at the vicissitudes of a world in which so much seems not only in transition but in decay, comfort themselves with the conception of a reality that is Pure and Abstract Form in which one may quietly be absorbed, a mind at peace with an equation. (The Realm of Essence, Santayana calls this Paradise of Forms, decked out in his jewelled and disillusioned prose.) Or they flee to the immutable principles of Thomism and the Catholic Church, or of Anglo-Catholicism, or Anglo-Communism, or to the authority of a political creed, of the Right or the Left, whose principles are beyond criticism and, even more important, beyond change. Time is the destroyer; let us destroy Time!

I even knew one young man who here, right in the heart of Manhattan, had made himself, for three years, into an Eastern mystic. He had tried all the other escapes from the world and from himself, and finally found a Buddhist monastery conducted in an apartment in the center of New York, where he lived, with some success, the life of detachment and peace. It is possible, I suppose, even at the present time, by a combination of luck and diligence, intellectual sensibility and spiritual courage—or callousness?—to find a bomb-proof shelter of the spirit. In the very capital of one of the sources of the uneasiness of the world, Rome, Santayana lives at present, communing with Essences. In the noise of the traffic of New York, and amid the current fashions of ideas and the current plight of the unemployed, it is possible (given economic security), to be a Buddhist of detachment. Men have achieved this before. Spinoza lived, too, in a time of unrest and trouble in the world, and managed, while he ground lenses for a living and while alien armies entered Holland, to keep his mind fixed on the eternal principles of understanding and of nature understood.

But I suspect a certain self-consciousness and uneasiness about people who feel the "changeless things" now. The uneasiness is largely a moral one. It seems either trivial or callous to play with metaphysics or to listen to fugues or to bathe in Brahms while the world is going to smash. The bombs descend on Barcelona and Madrid and on Hankow, but their detonations reach everywhere, into the Ivory Tower itself. There are other concerns in the world than civil liberty and economic justice, but even the inhabitants of the Ivory Tower know their own tenure of it is insecure unless those foundations are in order.

One of the dangers, indeed, is that our ears are becoming so attuned to detonations that we now mistake fireworks for real artillery. There is a lot of distracted busybodiness that passes for seriousness and good works. We smile at the leisurely Victorian lady who, having nothing else to do, did charity among her poorer neighbours. There is not a little among the connoisseurs of human misery that is equivalent to the Victorian busybody. One of the major exercises of social-minded New Yorkers of late has been to sign petitions, to attend meetings, to issue manifestos, to join organizations destined to stop the evils and violences of this world. Their efforts are often not much more than little twitterings against the throwers of bombs and the wreckers of human life and peace. The Victorian lady was carrying baskets of food and wine to alleviate distress caused by a ruthless new industrial system of which she and her own relatives were the beneficiaries. So too the contemporary reformers. These little manifestos and peace societies and leagues against this and that monstrosity in the world are symptoms of a real unrest. They are symptoms, too, of stabs, albeit random hysterical ones, against injustice; no less often they are mere self-expression on the part of their framers. I have signed a good many petitions in the past decade (though less than the number I have been asked to). After a time one wonders what this sharpshooting against evil amounts to. But, on the other hand, if it should really become epidemic to be concerned about the removable evils of the world, they might disappear. There is, despite the smug and the hopeless, nothing about the nature of the cosmos which makes it inevitable that there must be demagogues and wars and unemployed and diseases of malnutrition and starvation wages in the world. Petitions are mere twitterings, but they may be a prelude to something louder and more powerful, the concerted strength of men of goodwill.

Meanwhile it is fashionable, among those earnestly concerned to make the world if not better at least less disgusting, to sneer at the Ivory Tower. The inhabitants of that citadel (when they are not too precious) have as good a case in the long run as the earnest saviours of society whom one hears at meetings or in salons or on organizing committees. It is indeed much easier to scoff at the æsthetes and the detached philosophers in our time than to belittle those trying to moderate its worst bestialities. It does seem callous or silly to spend one's life trying to have as an ideal Pater's recommendation to "discern in the light on the hills a tone lovelier than the rest," or speculating on the nature of truth. There are women and children being bombed in Barcelona and in China; families starving in the deep South, and not only there; millions of refugees from the barbarisms of Central Europe who must be taken care of, and at once. It is, moreover, only a little less urgent that there be some co-operative front to insure that these things shall not recur, or there will be no refuges from barbarism anywhere.

I have been given moral pause by these facts, no less than many others whose instinctive preferences are for art and philosophy. There have been evenings when, among a group dedicated to cleansing revolution or obsessed by the miseries of our time, I have felt it were a form of debauchery or decadence to think about Spinoza or to listen to Haydn. There is nothing like a committee devoted to social good works to make one feel that one is an amateur Nero fiddling while Rome is burning. I have known any number of people committed to earnest saving of society, through violence or through discussion. I have known some of them well and knew them once as pupils. I have not been able to refrain from wondering what they expected or hoped life to be like when the last barricade had been taken, when the dust had settled down, the tumult had died, the blood forgotten, the last unearned increment expropriated, and the bastions of the co-operative commonwealth set up. Surely life will be there to be lived, after any not impossible revolution, just as it is now. Its justification will be then, as on any, save theological, assumption it is now, only in the opportunities it provides for enjoyment and understanding. Even the most ideal tomorrow will in its turn have to be a today, and then the doctrine of even the doctrinaires of the Ivory Tower will, perhaps, be proved to have had a point.

A parable, which happens to have happened, comes to my mind. A number of years ago I was visiting in the apartment of some good friends and good souls whose hearts were with the workers and whose comfortable apartment faced the river. It was during the worst of the depression on a winter day. There entered a charming lady with a melodious voice and handsome furs. As she drew off her gloves she said: "It's lovely the patterns the snow makes against the trees. What a splendid view you do have." "But have we a right to enjoy it," said my hostess with troubled seriousness, "when there are so many unemployed?" Then she added, as a relieving afterthought, and her face lighted up with moral relief: "But it will make work for some of them." Her conscience quieted, she resumed pouring tea.

In the twenties there were scornful jests made about the traditional Puritans who denied the natural impulses and obvious goods of earthly life. Many would rather have been found murdering their grandmothers than displaying an ascetic scruple about lust or gaiety, or a check upon present pleasures, however trifling, in the glum interest of Social Duty or some distant good. In the thirties Puritanism itself, with a new language, has become again a vogue (a vogue crossed at moments by a determination, itself puritanical, to stress the Importance of Living). For many with the future looming before us so ominous and desperate, it seems illicit to enjoy the present at all. Yet surely—a philosopher on holiday may be pardoned for making it a busman's holiday and indulging in argument—the quality of life is the ultimate aim of any way of living. However life be defined, it is something immediately sensed and felt and known. The desperate uneasiness of our lives (the insecurity is moral even where it is not economic) has brought it about that many people one meets have a scorn for the simple or the ultimate things which alone prevent living from being a harried road to nowhere. The sun still shines though we are in the sunset of an age, and the fact that there is barbarism rampant in the world is itself a challenge to understanding. One of the tragic destructions effected by the bombs, and a reason for nourishing the delicate and the best, is that they are destroying the peace, the clarity, and the sense of proportion of places and persons far beyond their physical range. The goods of life are not evil because they are insecure. Friends do not cease to be precious because the age is torn with enmities, and because there is gathering darkness we should not put out all lights.

I think of another parable, also one that occurred. I dined once with, and at the expense of, a wealthy revolutionary who loved the luxuries and amenities and shared them with his friends. This evening he had provided among other things caviare and champagne. He raised his glass. "After the revolution," he said, "everyone will have this. Here's to the simple life, champagne without sugar, caviare without salt." Champagne and caviare are not the only enjoyments, and it does not matter, I suppose, that they will never be available to everybody. But the exuberance and luxury of life of which they have become (falsely, I think) symbols are not impossible in an ordered society and are, within limits, available even now at times to some. The denial of happiness to oneself, the moral disapproval of it for others, does not improve the world; it robs it of an image of what living ideally should be. There is a kind of champagne in existence now; it is called Art. In music, in poetry, in drama, in the dance, chaos becomes momentarily order, and experience for the time being becomes pure vitality. The crowd who flocked to hear Bach at the W.P.A. concerts, including many who had no merely fashionable reason for showing an interest in music, is testimony that that champagne need be no impossible luxury, and that it demands no coteries and no affectation of taste. Philosophy itself is a kind of caviare (and not only caviare to the general) even now. It is a luxury of understanding. Many people, unfamiliar with the lingo of the schools or the cliques, love art in the sense of loving life where it is at once rich and clear. Everyone is a philosopher when he takes the time and fulfils the desire to stand apart, if only for a moment and if only superficially, to behold and to understand. One basks in the sun, one listens to music, one has friends, one broods, one wonders, and occasionally one is lighted with a gleam of understanding. Life becomes, even in a troubled and anxious period, for brief times, a joy merely to participate in, in love or friendship; to behold, in art; or, less often, a joy, tinctured with sadness, to understand. But in a society where the bombs batter against the mood of felicity, art and philosophy must, for the most part, be moral holidays.

Anyone who has the ambition, always a little impudent, to identify himself with the noble pursuit of philosophy, doubtless has no right to a moral holiday. It is his obligation to clarify to himself, and to others, so far as he can, the principles involved in the troubled issues of our generation. It is his task, even (not without the reservations imposed by modesty), to commit himself as to what is the good life. That his view of the good life will not be everyone's is not the point. It is his business to give what issues from his own honest attempt at understanding. But philosophy in some degree has always been, and always will be, a moral holiday. In philosophy profession and holiday are—or should be— one. To everyone, when the pressure of need or anxiety is temporarily reduced, life becomes a sequence of images, especially when time permits the bitter-sweet luxury of retrospect. The artist projects such images in words, on canvas, in marble, or translates their melodious incidence upon him into sound. A philosopher, dwelling with fondness and irony upon images thrown up by the past, cannot help dwelling if only by intimation on the principles which they illustrate. My images have risen in an age when the bombs, actual and moral, of contemporary life call one from contemplative dreaming. But even amid the distractions, one must retreat to the Ivory Tower for refreshment or for understanding. Dwelling there for the time being, one is perhaps deserting the realm of philosophy for that of poetry, and exact analysis for the pleasures of a waking dream. But philosophy and poetry, as some have maintained, are not very far from each other. I have simply put down some scattered images of my own waking dream, in which, whether in Syria or in Manhattan, among friends of my childhood in New York or among older friends there or abroad or in other parts of the country, or among the

genial forms of art, I have seemed to sense the same perplexed and dreaming spirit of man. The itinerant humanist
is bound to recognize, amid whatever diversities of setting,
the same human spirit. For even in our age, to the friendly
observer, that spirit, struggling to the light amid the thorns,
however blindly or perversely, still must seem human. And
despite the rising tide of barbarism, I cannot help thinking
(though it be the residue of that hopeful Liberalism current
among the young before the war) the distinctive humanity
of men will survive.

Looking back over these pages, I recall that I had promised
the reader simply images of persons and places, with an
allusion now and again to the principles which they seemed
to me to illustrate. I also promised him that this book would
not be an autobiography. But one who has been a professional philosopher by trade cannot help carrying some
traces of his *métier* with him, even on a holiday. As for autobiography—how is one to report his experience of persons
and places and ideas, without telling something of the circumstances in which they appeared as images to him? In
telling of the environment of things remembered, the re-
memberer cannot, I fear, hide himself. I note thus (with
embarrassment) that, despite my good intentions, some
autobiography, chronologically in disarray, has crept into
these pages, and (to reverse Samuel Johnson's remark) I
have found that, despite a relatively cheerful disposition,
philosophy keeps breaking in. I can only say in extenuation
that I have selected only such items of my own history as
seemed necessary to tell of other persons and things. Compared, moreover, with the elaborate paraphernalia and the

esoteric issues that are commonly called philosophy in professional circles, such meditations as have crept into these
pages are the veriest holiday triflings. But in comparison with
the final truth of things which a god might know, even the
most serious philosophy would seem a child's play too.